	DATE DUE		

The Assyrian Empire

Titles in the World History Series

The Age of Augustus
The Age of Feudalism
The Age of Pericles
The Alamo
America in the 1960s
The American Frontier
The American Revolution
Ancient Greece
The Ancient Near East
Architecture
The Assyrian Empire
Aztec Civilization
The Battle of the
  Little Bighorn
The Black Death
The Byzantine Empire
Caesar's Conquest of Gaul
The California Gold Rush
The Chinese Cultural
  Revolution
The Civil Rights Movement
The Collapse of the
  Roman Republic
The Conquest of Mexico
The Creation of Israel
The Crimean War
The Crusades
The Cuban Missile Crisis
The Cuban Revolution
The Decline and Fall of the
  Roman Empire
The Early Middle Ages
Egypt of the Pharaohs
Elizabethan England
The End of the Cold War
The French and
  Indian War
The French Revolution
The Glorious Revolution
The Great Depression

Greek and Roman
  Mythology
Greek and Roman Science
Greek and Roman Theater
The History of Slavery
Hitler's Reich
The Hundred Years' War
The Industrial Revolution
The Inquisition
The Italian Renaissance
The Late Middle Ages
The Lewis and Clark
  Expedition
The Mexican Revolution
The Mexican War of
  Independence
Modern Japan
The Mongol Empire
The Persian Empire
The Punic Wars
The Reformation
The Relocation of the
  North American Indian
The Renaissance
The Roaring Twenties
The Roman Empire
The Roman Republic
Roosevelt and the New Deal
The Russian Revolution
Russia of the Tsars
The Scientific Revolution
The Spread of Islam
The Stone Age
Traditional Africa
Traditional Japan
The Travels of Marco Polo
Twentieth Century Science
The Wars of the Roses
The Watts Riot
Women's Suffrage

WORLD HISTORY SERIES ■ ■ ■

The Assyrian Empire

by
Don Nardo

Lucent Books, P.O. Box 289011, San Diego, CA 92198-9011

Library of Congress Cataloging-in-Publication Data

Nardo, Don, 1947–
     The Assyrian Empire / by Don Nardo.
          p.   cm. — (World history series)
     Includes bibliographical references and index.
     Summary: Discusses the history of the Assyrian Empire,
including its early people, the rise of the Assyrian nation, its
rebirth, the empire at its height, and the nation's collapse.
     ISBN 1-56006-313-0 (lib. : alk. paper)
     1. Assyria—History—Juvenile literature. [1. Assyria—
History.] I. Title. II. Series.
DS73.2.N37   1998
935'.03—dc21   97-50166
                                                                          CIP
                                                                           AC

Contents

Foreword

Each year on the first day of school, nearly every history teacher faces the task of explaining why his or her students should study history. One logical answer to this question is that exploring what happened in our past explains how the things we often take for granted—our customs, ideas, and institutions—came to be. As statesman and historian Winston Churchill put it, "Every nation or group of nations has its own tale to tell. Knowledge of the trials and struggles is necessary to all who would comprehend the problems, perils, challenges, and opportunities which confront us today." Thus, a study of history puts modern ideas and institutions in perspective. For example, though the founders of the United States were talented and creative thinkers, they clearly did not invent the concept of democracy. Instead, they adapted some democratic ideas that had originated in ancient Greece and with which the Romans, the British, and others had experimented. An exploration of these cultures, then, reveals their very real connection to us through institutions that continue to shape our daily lives.

Another reason often given for studying history is the idea that lessons exist in the past from which contemporary societies can benefit and learn. This idea, although controversial, has always been an intriguing one for historians. Those who agree that society can benefit from the past often quote philosopher George Santayana's famous statement, "Those who cannot remember the past are condemned to repeat it." Historians who subscribe to Santayana's philosophy believe that, for example, studying the events that led up to the major world wars or other significant historical events would allow society to chart a different and more favorable course in the future.

Just as difficult as convincing students to realize the importance of studying history is the search for useful and interesting supplementary materials that present historical events in a context that can be easily understood. The volumes in Lucent Books' World History Series attempt to present a broad, balanced, and penetrating view of the march of history. Ancient Egypt's important wars and rulers, for example, are presented against the rich and colorful backdrop of Egyptian religious, social, and cultural developments. The series engages the reader by enhancing historical events with these cultural contexts. For example, in *Ancient Greece*, the text covers the role of women in that society. Slavery is discussed in *The Roman Empire*, as well as how slaves earned their freedom. The numerous and varied aspects of everyday life in these and other societies are explored in each volume of the series. Additionally, the series covers the major political, cultural, and philosophical ideas as the torch of civilization is passed from ancient Mesopotamia and Egypt, through Greece, Rome, Medieval Europe, and other world cultures, to the modern day.

The material in the series is formatted in a thorough, precise, and organized manner. Each volume offers the reader a comprehensive and clearly written overview of an important historical event or period. The topic under discussion is placed in a broad historical context. For example, *The Italian Renaissance* begins with a discussion of the High Middle Ages and the loss of central control that allowed certain Italian cities to develop artistically. The book ends by looking forward to the Reformation and interpreting the societal changes that grew out of the Renaissance. Thus, students are not only involved in an historical era, but also enveloped by the events leading up to that era and the events following it.

One important and unique feature in the World History Series is the primary and secondary source quotations that richly supplement each volume. These quotes are useful in a number of ways. First, they allow students access to sources they would not normally be exposed to because of the difficulty and obscurity of the original source. The quotations range from interesting anecdotes to farsighted cultural perspectives and are drawn from historical witnesses both past and present. Second, the quotes demonstrate how and where historians themselves derive their information on the past as they strive to reach a consensus on historical events. Lastly, all of the quotes are footnoted, familiarizing students with the citation process and allowing them to verify quotes and/or look up the original source if the quote piques their interest.

Finally, the books in the World History Series provide a detailed launching point for further research. Each book contains a bibliography specifically geared toward student research. A second, annotated bibliography introduces students to all the sources the author consulted when compiling the book. A chronology of important dates gives students an overview, at a glance, of the topic covered. Where applicable, a glossary of terms is included.

In short, the series is designed not only to acquaint readers with the basics of history, but also to make them aware that their lives are a part of an ongoing human saga. Perhaps they will then come to the same realization as famed historian Arnold Toynbee. In his monumental work, *A Study of History*, he wrote about becoming aware of history flowing through him in a mighty current, and of his own life "welling like a wave in the flow of this vast tide."

Important Dates in the History of the Assyrian Empire

B.C.   ca. 5500   ca. 2400–2200   ca. 1813–1781   ca. 1600   ca. 1365–1330   ca. 1200

B.C.

ca. 5500
People from the upland areas surrounding the Mesopotamian plains begin to descend from the hills and settle in the Tigris and Euphrates River valleys.

ca. 3300–3000
The Sumerians build the first Mesopotamian cities, in the plain just north-west of the Persian Gulf; the Sumerians also begin using a complex writing system that evolves into what modern scholars call cuneiform.

ca. 2400–2200
Akkadian rulers, most prominent among them King Sargon, conquer Sumeria and unite north-ern and southern Meso-potamia.

ca. 2000
An unknown Babylonian scribe collects the epic tales of the early Mesopo-tamian hero Gilgamesh; the Sumerian language has by now ceased to be spoken and is used only by priest-scholars.

ca. 1813–1781
Reign of Shamshi-Adad, founder of Assyria's first great royal dynasty and the first of that nation's rulers about whom any details are known.

ca. 1759
Babylonian king Ham-murabi conquers the kingdom of Mari, on the upper Euphrates, and soon afterward absorbs Assur and the other Assyrian cities.

ca. 1600
Babylon is sacked by the Hittites, an ambitious people from central Anatolia (Asia Minor).

ca. 1600–1365
First Mesopotamian dark age, during which Assyria is dominated first by the Kassite rulers of Baby-lonia and then by the kingdom of Mitanni, centered on the upper Tigris.

ca. 1365–1330
Reign of Assuruballit I, first king of the newly independent Assyria.

ca. 1244–1208
Reign of Tukulti-Ninurta I, who captures the city of Babylon.

ca. 1200
Many Near Eastern and Mediterranean cities are sacked and burned, including those of the Hittites, as the region undergoes catastrophic upheaval, the causes of which remain unclear; Assyria largely escapes the destruction, leaving it the lone surviving great power in the western Near Eastern sphere.

ca. 1115–1077
Reign of Tiglathpileser I, whose armies reach the coast of the Mediter-ranean Sea and receive tribute from Byblos and other Phoenician cities.

ca. 1070–911
Second Mesopotamian dark age, in which the Assyrian realm drastically shrinks in size and power and is politically and mil-itarily quiescent.

ca. 911–891
Reign of Adad-Nirari II, first king of the newly revived Assyria, which now enters its greatest age of expansion and glory.

ca. 883–859
Reign of Assurnasirpal II, who repeats his ancestor Tiglathpileser's feat of reaching the Mediterranean coast.

ca. 853
Assyrian king Shalamaneser III fights the allied forces of Damascus, Israel, and other coastal kingdoms at Qarqar, on the Orontes River north of Damascus; unable to defeat them, he withdraws.

ca. 744–727
Reign of Tiglathpileser III, who reasserts Assyrian domination of Syria and Palestine, taking Damascus and annexing half of Israel.

ca. 722–705
Reign of Sargon II, founder of the Sargonid dynasty, who crushes numerous rebellions and builds a new royal palace at Dur-Sharrukin, northeast of Nineveh.

ca. 694
Sargon's successor, Sennacherib, destroys Babylon.

ca. 681
Sennacherib is assassinated by his own sons; one of them, Esarhaddon, ascends the throne and soon begins rebuilding Babylon.

ca. 671
Esarhaddon invades Egypt, taking the capital, Memphis; Egypt later rebels and Esarhaddon dies while on his way to put down the insurrection.

ca. 668–627
Reign of Assurbanipal, who inherits the Assyrian Empire at its height of power.

ca. 639
Assurbanipal destroys Assyria's longtime foe, the kingdom of Elam, situated east of the Mesopotamian plains.

627
Assurbanipal dies and Assyria is wracked by civil war.

626
Chaldean ruler Nabopolassar seizes Babylon and launches a war against the weakened Assyria.

615
Media's King Cyaxares attacks Assyria from the east; the following year he captures and sacks Assur, the most sacred of Assyria's cities; Cyaxares and Nabopolassar form an anti-Assyrian alliance.

612
A combined Babylonian-Median army ravages the Assyrian heartland, destroying Nimrud and Nineveh.

610
The Babylonians and Medes defeat the last Assyrian ruler near Harran, on the upper reaches of the Euphrates; the Assyrian nation now ceases to exist.

A People Who Lived and Died by the Sword

To the modern world before the mid–nineteenth century, the name of Assyria, which had once struck terror into the hearts of millions, was nothing more than a term occasionally mentioned in the Bible and the books of a few ancient Greek and Roman writers. According to these works, the Assyrians were one of several prosperous and powerful peoples who inhabited the Tigris and Euphrates River valleys in biblical times. This central and then very fertile region of the Near East is often referred to as Mesopotamia, a term derived from Greek words meaning "the land between the rivers." Like the Babylonians and other legendary Mesopotamian cultures, the Assyrians had long ago vanished from history's stage; and modern historians had no way even to prove their existence, much less to locate their remains.

This lack of concrete evidence stemmed mainly from an unfortunate choice of building material. Unlike the Egyptians, Greeks, and Romans, who constructed many of their monuments of durable stone, the Mesopotamians built mostly in mud-brick, which disintegrates easily. The Near East's hot sun, periodic rains, annual floods, and shifting sands slowly leveled and buried the palaces and cities, leaving only shapeless earthen mounds. As the arid desert wastes reclaimed them, these sites lost their original identities; for more than two thousand years, their secrets remained concealed, even from the local descendants of those who had originally inhabited them.

The veil of secrecy shrouding Assyria and its sister cultures began to lift in the 1840s, as a series of young amateur archaeologists, mostly from France and England, rapidly uncovered one Assyrian palace and city after another. The most successful, famous, and influential of these excavators was an English civil servant and adventurer named Austen Henry Layard. On a clear and quiet early November night in 1845, the twenty-eight-year-old Layard sat in a tent in the desert in what is now northern Iraq, an area then under Turkish control. Too excited to sleep, he could think of nothing else but the huge, flat-topped, and mysterious earthen mound of Nimrud, beside which he was camped. Partly inspired by Frenchman Paul Émile Botta's recent discovery of an ancient Assyrian palace at Khorsabad, about fifty miles to the north, Layard had come to Nimrud hoping to find sculptures and other artifacts for the prestigious British Museum in London.

Layard's hope was transformed into reality in spectacular fashion on his very first day of digging. He and the six workmen he had hired from a local Arab chieftain began shoveling into the mound at dawn; and within twenty-four hours they had discovered rooms from two separate palaces, replete with magnificent sculptured wall reliefs. The young Englishman later described one of the vivid battle scenes depicted:

> Two chariots, drawn by horses . . . were each occupied by a group of three warriors; the principal person in both groups was beardless. . . . He was clothed in a complete suit of mail, and wore a pointed helmet on his head. . . . The left hand . . . grasped a bow at full stretch; whilst the right . . . held an arrow ready to be discharged. A second warrior with reins and whip urged to the utmost of their speed three horses, who were galloping over the plain. A third [figure], without helmet, and with flowing hair and beard, held a shield for the defense of the principal figure. Under the horses' feet . . . were the conquered, wounded by the arrows of the conquerors.[1]

As more buildings at Nimrud (ancient Kalhu), Nineveh, Assur, and other Assyrian sites came to light, Layard and his successors found thousands of similar sculptures, a significant portion of them depicting warriors, weapons, battles, sieges, and other military themes. This seemed to confirm what the Bible and other ancient works had said about the Assyrians—that they were the most warlike and feared of all ancient peoples. "Woe to the bloody city," wrote the Hebrew prophet Nahum about Nineveh, "all full of lies and booty."[2] "Behold," echoed another prophet, Isaiah, "you have heard what the kings of Assyria have done to all lands, destroying them utterly. . . . Of truth, O Lord, the kings of Assyria have laid waste all the nations and their lands, and have cast their gods into the fire."[3] And the fifth-century B.C. Greek historian Herodotus spoke of the Assyrians as having been "masters of upper Asia over a period of five hundred and twenty years," and of various peoples gallantly fighting to shake off "the Assyrian yoke and become a free people."[4]

A century and a half of excavation, supported by the translation of many Mesopotamian texts, has revealed that the Assyrians were not merely ruthless destroyers;

A drawing of a carved relief found at Nimrud, one of Assyria's chief cities, shows Assyrian warriors besieging an enemy fortress. A wheeled siege tower carries archers, and the fortress wall crumbles before a battering ram.

they were also prodigious builders, as the ruins of Nineveh and their other cities attest, as well as industrious farmers, traders, and skilled artists. Yet the evidence shows that, perhaps more than any other ancient nation, Assyria sustained itself through aggressive military raids, campaigns, and wars. And more often than not it treated those it conquered with a bloodthirsty cruelty almost unique in humanity's recorded annals. This harsh policy led the Assyrians to power and glory, as in the early centuries of the first millennium B.C. they created the world's first large empire. In a number of respects this realm became the model that later peoples, including the Persians, successfully copied in building their own empires. Moreover, by forcing the states of the Near East into a large-scale unity (albeit an unstable one), Assyria made it easier for later conquerors to do the same. The Assyrians' ruthlessness, noted historian Chester Starr points out,

shows the sternness required to break and harness the [human and national energies] of the Near East. The Assyrian period was in reality one of the greatest turning points in the civilized history of the area. The next great empire, the Persian, reaped the benefit and could afford to exercise its sway in a more lenient style.[5]

But the Assyrians' stern and brutal methods also inevitably led to their doom. As a matter of course, their soldiers committed one cold-blooded atrocity after another; and their kings proudly boasted of these deeds. "Many [of the defeated] I took as living captives," a ninth-century B.C. Assyrian monarch recorded in his annals.

From some I cut off their hands and their fingers, and from others I cut off their noses, their ears, and their fingers, of many I put out the eyes. I made one pillar [pile] of the living, and an-

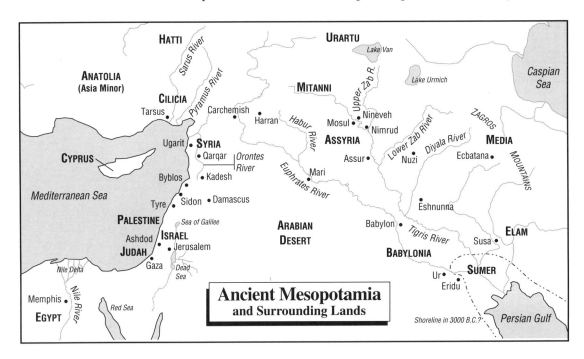

Ancient Mesopotamia
and Surrounding Lands

A fragment of an Assyrian wall relief depicts soldiers delivering captured enemy heads to scribes, whose tally of these grisly trophies and other information about a recent battle will be delivered to the king.

other of heads, and I bound their heads to posts [stakes] round about the city. Their young men and maidens I burned in the fire, the city I destroyed, I devastated, I burned it with fire and consumed it.[6]

Not surprisingly, such heinous acts made bitter enemies at every turn. Eventually, the strongest of these enemies banded together to rid the Near Eastern world of what all had come to see as its most deadly scourge; and just as Assyria had devastated and eradicated so many of its neighbors, that nation was itself finally and utterly erased from the windswept northern Mesopotamian plains.

In the epic sweep of the rise and fall of great peoples on those plains, the triumph and tragedy of the Assyrians stands out. A unique blend of heroic and horrific extremes, their story is perhaps history's classic example of a people who lived and subsequently died by the sword. "Assyria is there [in hell's pit]," the Hebrew God told the prophet Ezekiel, "and all her company . . . all of them slain, fallen by the sword . . . who spread terror in the land of the living."[7] Layard captured the tragic irony of Assyria's fall from the heights of imperial power to the depths of obscurity in a different way. Gazing on the huge stone torsos of winged lions that had guarded the portals of Nimrud's palaces, he remarked in hushed and wistful tones:

> For twenty-five centuries they had been hidden from the eye of man, and they now stood forth once more in their ancient majesty. But how changed was the scene around them! The luxury and civilization of a mighty nation had . . . been succeeded by ruins and shapeless heaps of earth. Above the spacious hall in which they stood, the plow had passed and the corn now waved.[8]

1 Between the Great Rivers: The Early Peoples of Mesopotamia

One of the great crossroads of the ancient world, the Near East, with the flat plains of Mesopotamia at its center, witnessed the incessant rise and fall of city-states, kingdoms, and great empires over the course of more than four thousand years. Among these empires, the Assyrian was one of the largest, longest lived, and most powerful, as well as *the* most feared. The success of Assyria and many other Near Eastern realms was significantly aided by the wide variety of terrains and climates in the area, which was bounded by the Arabian Desert and Persian Gulf in the south; the fertile Mediterranean coasts of Palestine and Syria in the west; the Black Sea, mountainous Armenia, and the Caspian Sea in the north; and the rugged highlands of the Zagros Mountains and Iranian plateau in the east. The lands enclosed by these natural barriers featured many local regions that were very hospitable to settlement and the growth of large local populations. According to the distinguished Assyriologist A. Leo Oppenheim:

> Along the rivers we find fertile, oasis-like stretches such as those that appear here and there on the Tigris [River] and its tributaries, and especially on the Euphrates [River], wherever the formation of the river banks makes agriculture by irrigation possible. The flatlands and the narrow valleys, between the parallel chains of hills which ascend in ever higher ranges from the piedmont plains along the Tigris to the alpine tops of the Zagros Mountains, enjoy sufficient rainfall to assure annual cereal crops and to produce an abundance of fruit trees. In the plain between and beyond the two great rivers are widely scattered areas where the local topography and the nature of the soil allow man . . . to raise cereals, although the crops vary considerably in yield and quality with the amount of rain and the care given the fields. Large tracts of land between the sown fields and the barren desert offer grazing grounds for flocks of sheep and goats, even for cattle, depending on the season and the region.[9]

It was in this extremely varied, attractive, and fertile region—composed of the Mesopotamian plains and the uplands surrounding them—that humankind's first true cities appeared.

Early Settlement of the Near East

These first cities were, naturally enough, preceded by villages and other much smaller settlements. For a long time, historians thought that the earliest, smallest, and simplest Near Eastern settlements had grown up on the alluvial plains of the great rivers. It is now clear, however, that this assumption was wrong and that the Near East's initial inhabited zone ran through the wide belt of foothills surrounding the Mesopotamian plains; this belt stretched in an arc from Palestine northward through Syria and eastern Anatolia (or Asia Minor, present-day Turkey), eastward across northern Iraq, and into the Iranian plateau. The growth of these settlements apparently coincided with (or was made possible by) the development of agriculture, perhaps as early as 9000 or 10,000 B.C. The inhabitants of the region, comments University of Oklahoma scholar Daniel Snell,

> learned that after a few years grains increased in size when human beings planted, tended, and harvested them. Animals too changed some of their characteristics when they were domesticated, and both animals and plants were more convenient for people and more reliable than they had been before people were planting and managing them.[10]

Simply put, agriculture and herding provided more food, which in turn stimulated population growth and increased the size and complexity of human settlements.

By the eighth millennium B.C., some of these settlements had begun to protect themselves with defensive walls of brick and stone. The most famous early example is the town of Jericho, in the Jordan valley in Palestine, featuring stone defenses enclosing an area of eleven acres. A larger fortified village, covering some thirty-two acres, flourished in the seventh and sixth millennia B.C. at Çatal Hüyük in southeastern Anatolia. The town's "square, flat-roofed houses," writes noted archaeologist Dr. Trevor Watkins,

> were built side by side like a pile of children's building blocks, pushed together. Access to each house was by means of a door at roof-level, from which a steep ladder led down into the living area. Circulation [movement] around the settlement was across the flat roofs. The edge of such a settlement would have presented a solid, blank wall to any intruder or attacker. Once the ladders . . . were drawn up, the settlement would have been impregnable.[11]

Çatal Hüyük's military defenses were likely designed to keep out local bands of marauders; however, they foreshadowed the large-scale international warfare that characterized the area later, especially in the second millennium B.C. when it was part of the Hittite Empire, which vied with Assyria for dominance.

The Sumerian City-States

Eventually, perhaps by 5500 B.C. or so, the population of the upland regions had grown great enough to stimulate expansion southward into the Tigris and Euphrates plains. "People may have perceived that their villages were getting too crowded," Snell suggests, "even if they may not have been crowded at all by later standards. And so they moved out into the forbidding frontier area, which turned out to be extremely productive agriculturally."[12] However, successful agriculture on the plains required considerably more work than it had in the hills, where rainfall was sufficient to water the crops. The plains were more arid, and people had to develop techniques for large-scale irrigation. Fortunately, the Euphrates is a calm and slow-moving river that is relatively easy to divert into smaller channels, and a network of lush fields and prosperous villages rapidly grew along the riverbanks.[13]

Mesopotamia's Two Great Rivers

In this excerpt from his book Ancient Mesopotamia: Portrait of a Dead Civilization, *distinguished Assyriologist A. Leo Oppenheim explains how the courses and annual floodings of the Tigris and Euphrates Rivers affected patterns of settlement and farming in the region.*

"The Tigris and Euphrates both descend from the Armenian mountains, fed by a number of mountain streams. The courses of some of these tributaries are, at one place, only fifteen miles apart, making it thus practically impossible to reach Mesopotamia without crossing either the Tigris or the Euphrates. After breaking through the last hills, the courses differ widely in direction and character. The Tigris flows swiftly east and then southeast parallel to the Zagros ranges, passing near Nineveh, Nimrud, and Assur—all three capitals of successive Assyrian empires. . . . Downstream its course underwent many changes in the historic period, which prevented the growth of permanent settlements on its banks. . . . Quite different is the course of the Euphrates. When it leaves the mountains it runs southwest and reaches a point where only ninety miles separate it from the Mediterranean Sea. Then it turns south in a wide bend and . . . eventually southeast. . . . It reaches the alluvial plain at Hit, near the Tigris. . . . Annual flooding is characteristic of both rivers and deeply influenced all life in [the region]. . . . The two rivers follow a similar pattern: autumn rains in the uplands cause a general swelling of the water through the winter and spring till the melting snow in the Armenian mountains makes the crest of the flood reach the plains in April and May. . . . Since the flood stage is reached so late in the season in Mesopotamia, it was essential to prepare dikes and levees to protect the green fields from the water. . . . Equally important, the late flooding increased the tendency of the soil toward salinization [increase in salt content]. . . . This progressive salinization of irrigated soil cuts down its yield . . . [necessitating] the relocation of agricultural territories."

The identities of these first river peoples remain unknown, in large part because they left behind few artifacts and no written records. The first important identifiable people in the area were the Sumerians, who inhabited the flatlands of southern Mesopotamia just northwest of the Persian Gulf at least by the late fourth millennium B.C.[14] Exactly who the Sumerians were and where they came from is uncertain, and these questions constitute the kernel of what historians often refer to as the "Sumerian problem." Some scholars think they were the descendants of the original hill peoples who migrated onto the plains beginning in the sixth millennium; others contend that the Sumerians migrated into the Near East in the fourth millennium from the east, possibly from India. The second argument appears to be the stronger; for the Sumerian language was different than the one originally spoken in Mesopotamia, revealed by the fact that important place-names in the area, such as Ur, Eridu, and Uruk, are not Sumerian; in fact, Sumerian is unlike any other known tongue, living or dead.

Whatever the Sumerians' origins may have been, they, along with the ancient Egyptians in the Nile River valley, are credited with two major milestones in the development of civilization. The first of these was the creation of cities and city-states. The first cities appeared in Sumer shortly before 3000 B.C. Perhaps the first full-fledged city was Eridu, then located very near the shore of the Persian Gulf (which has since that time receded about 125 miles southeastward). The Sumerians believed the city was the site of the original mound of creation, the original land that rose from the sea at the beginning of time. Supposedly, Eridu was also the home of

An ancient Mesopotamian statue, made of terracotta and dating from the late third or early second millenium B.C., depicts a shepherd carrying a lamb.

the first king and the first civilized arts and works, among these the Apsu, the most ancient shrine in Sumer, dwelling place of Enki, god of the primeval waters and of wisdom. Other early important cities included Ur, a few miles north of Eridu; Lagash, some fifty miles to the northwest; and strung out toward the northwest—Larsa, Uruk, and Nippur. These had begun as small villages, probably, like Jericho and Çatal Hüyük, covering only a few dozen acres at most. Under the Sumerians, however, their size increased manyfold. Between 3000 and 2700 B.C., for example, Uruk became a city of tens of thousands of inhabitants enclosed by a circuit wall six miles in circumference.

These early cities, like all in Mesopotamia for hundreds of years to come,

Known as the Royal Standard of Ur, this famous panel, found in a grave dated to ca. 2600 B.C., shows the people of Ur bringing tribute to their king. The mosaics are of shell and red limestone set on lapis lazuli (a blue semiprecious stone).

were not dependent units within a larger Sumerian nation, but rather independent city-states, each in a sense a tiny national unit in its own right. In the third millennium B.C., a typical Mesopotamian city-state consisted of a densely populated central town surrounded by dependent villages and farmland. About their size and setup, historian Michael Wood writes:

> A big city-state like Lagash had 36,000 male adults, Uruk perhaps the same. They were closely organized and controlled. In Nippur at a later period, there were 200 subsidiary villages in its territory, clustered around five main canals and sixty lesser ones, joined by a web of countless small irrigation ditches, all of which were subject to rules, duties and control. . . . As for the physical make-up of the city itself . . . Uruk was one-third built up [with homes and shops], one-third gardens, [and] one-third temple property. . . . The design of houses . . . was identical to that used [in the area] up till the advent of air conditioning, with central courtyards, windcatchers, and

serdabs (sunken rooms) to keep the ferocious summer heat at bay.[15]

The Invention and Spread of Writing

The other major civilized advance credited to the Sumerians was the development of writing, an invention that quickly spread to other parts of the Near East. Sometime between 3300 and 3000 B.C., a complex writing system appeared, the earliest examples of which have been found in the ruins of Uruk. Scribes pressed pointed sticks, styluses, or other objects into moist clay tablets; when the tablets dried and hardened, they became cumbersome but permanent records, the world's first versions of letters, account sheets, and books. In its most mature form, this writing system consisted mainly of small wedge-shaped marks arranged in various combinations. Modern scholars dubbed it "cuneiform" after the Latin word *cuneus,* meaning wedge- or nail-shaped. There were between five hundred and six hundred separate cuneiform signs in all, requiring a great deal of time and effort to master, so it is likely that only a handful of scribes and other highly educated people could read and write.

Of the thousands of cuneiform tablets discovered since the mid-1800s, the vast majority consist of dry administrative and financial records, including bills, accounts received, inventories, volumes of barley or other foodstuffs, and measures of land parcels. Though monotonous, these reveal much about social customs and economic practices, especially among members of the upper classes, who owned the land and controlled commerce. On the other hand, some tablets preserve actual literature, the most important examples being the creation myths that became the common heritage of all Mesopotamian peoples, including the Assyrians.

The most famous and influential of these myths appear in the *Epic of Gilgamesh.* This large compilation of early heroic tales and folklore, first collected into a unified whole circa 2000 B.C. by an unknown Babylonian scribe, centers on the exploits of the title character, who was probably origi-

Sumerian characters on a brick dating from about 2500 B.C. record the building of a religious temple by one of the kings of the prosperous city of Ur.

nally a real Sumerian ruler.[16] Gilgamesh searches long and hard for the secret of eternal life, only to find in the end that no human can escape old age and death. Along the way he has many adventures, including a meeting with Utnapishtim (whom the Sumerians called Ziusudra), who tells him the story of the great flood, an attempt by the gods to "destroy the seed of humanity." Warned of the impending deluge by the god Ea, Utnapishtim builds a great ark. "All that I had I loaded onto her," he recalls. "All that I had of living beings of all kinds I loaded on her. I brought to the ship all my family and household; cattle . . . [and] beasts of the field, all the workmen I brought on board." Then the flood strikes, destroying humanity and leaving the landscape "level as a flat roof." Finally, the ark comes to rest on a mountaintop protruding from the floodwaters.

> When the seventh day arrived, I sent forth a dove, letting it free. . . . Not finding a resting place, it came back. I sent forth a swallow. . . . Not finding a resting place, it came back. I sent forth a raven. . . . The raven went and saw the decrease of the waters. It ate, croaked, but did not turn back. Then I let all [on board the ark] out to the four regions [of the earth, i.e., the Near East, then the known world] and brought an offering [sacrifice to the gods].[17]

As is well known, more than a thousand years later the Hebrew scribes who compiled the books of the biblical Old Testament included their own version of this flood tale, changing the name of the ark's builder to Noah. Other elements and motifs of the Gilgamesh story later filtered out of the Near East, cropping up in the Greek

Homeric epics, the *Iliad* and *Odyssey,* and, with Islamic colorings, in the Arabic *Thousand and One Nights.*

A drawing of an alabaster sculpture depicting the Mesopotamian hero Gilgamesh, said to have survived the great flood.

Religion and Language

Like its cuneiform writing and epic literature, Sumer's gods and religious customs spread throughout Mesopotamia and other parts of the Near East, becoming more or less universal and surviving long after the Sumerians themselves had disappeared. Noted scholar of Mesopotamian culture Georges Roux explains:

> For more than three thousand years the religious ideas promoted by the Sumerians played an extraordinary part in the public and private life of the Mesopotamians, modeling their institutions, coloring their works of art and literature, pervading every form of activity from the highest functions of the kings to the day-to-day occupations of their subjects. . . . The fact that Sumerian society crystallized around temples . . . had deep and lasting consequences. In theory, for instance, the land never ceased to belong to the gods, and the mighty Assyrian monarchs whose empire extended from the Nile to the Caspian Sea [in the early seventh century B.C.] were the humble servants of their god Assur, just as the governors of Lagash, who ruled over a few square miles of Sumer, were those of their god Ningersu.[18]

The most revered of the Sumerian gods were An (or Anu, whose main temple was in Uruk), sovereign of the universe; Enlil (his worship centered in Nippur), creator and ruler of earth; Enki, god of the waters; and Enzu, Utu, and Inanna (or Ninni), deities of the moon, sun, and planet Venus, respectively. The Babylonians, Assyrians, and other peoples who suc-

The Creation of Gilgamesh's Nemesis

In this excerpt from the Epic of Gilgamesh *(quoted from James B. Pritchard's* Ancient Near Eastern Texts Relating to the Old Testament*), the gods create Enkidu, a powerful wild man, to check Gilgamesh's despotic rule of the Sumerian city of Uruk.*

"The nobles of Uruk are gloomy in their chambers: 'Gilgamesh leaves not the son to his father; day and night is his arrogance unbridled. He should be our shepherd: strong, stately, and wise!' . . . The gods harkened to their plea. . . . The great Aruru they called: 'You, Aruru, did create Gilgamesh; create now his double; his stormy heart let it match.' . . . Aruru washed her hands, pinched off clay and cast it on the steppe [plain]. On the steppe she created valiant Enkidu. . . . Shaggy with hair is his whole body, he is endowed with head hair like a woman. . . . He knows neither people nor land. . . . With the gazelles he feeds on grass, with the wild beasts he jostles at the watering-place, with the teeming creatures his heart delights in water."

ceeded the Sumerians in the region and adopted their culture also borrowed these gods, sometimes changing their names. Thus, Enki became Ea, Enzu became Sin, Utu became Shamash, and Inanna became Ishtar in later Mesopotamian pantheons. At the same time, the Babylonians identified their chief god Marduk and the Assyrians their god Assur with the Sumerian Enlil. These gods, like those of the later Greeks and Romans, were seen as having human form as well as human qualities, frailties, and passions. "In brief," says Roux, "they represented the best and worst of human nature on a superhuman scale."[19]

The Sumerian language also survived Sumer's political decline in the late third millennium B.C. Although Sumerian was no longer widely spoken after 2000 B.C., it survived as a sort of sacred literary language, just as Latin became for the Catholic Church and the European scholarly community after it ceased to be spoken. The spoken language that immediately replaced Sumerian throughout Mesopotamia was Akkadian, a Semitic tongue related to Hebrew and Arabic. Akkadian speakers had long inhabited the central and northern reaches of the Tigris-Euphrates plains, and they eventually gained dominance over the Sumerian city-states in the south. The Akkadians easily adopted the Sumerians' cuneiform writing system to their own tongue, which shows that system's flexibility, since the two languages are as different from each other as Latin is from Chinese.

It must be stressed that the Akkadians were not a separate racial, ethnic, or social group. "Ethnic divisions played little part in major ancient Near Eastern societies," states H. W. F. Saggs, an expert on ancient languages.

A Babylonian tablet, dating from the ninth century B.C., shows the sun god, Shamash, receiving homage from three worshipers. The emblem of the solar disk can be seen on the altar.

This is very clear for Mesopotamia. The third millennium B.C. knew no split on racial lines between the speakers of different languages, and no such split developed later. The cultural pressure of Mesopotamian society ensured that although many diverse ethnic groups entered Mesopotamia, all were eventually assimilated, and none permanently stood apart.[20]

Warfare and Conquest

Language, then, was the main cultural difference between the Akkadians and those peoples they conquered, among them the Sumerians. The transition from independent city-states to nations and empires begins with these Akkadian conquests, which occurred between 2400 and 2200 B.C. Initially, a number of Akkadian rulers managed to unite the central Mesopotamian cities into a national unit; then the first great imperialist, Sargon of Akkad (or Agade), attacked and absorbed the Sumerian cities, his armies marching all the way to the Persian Gulf. For the first time in history, the lower and upper halves of Mesopotamia, bound before only by religious, social, and other cultural ties, were united as a single nation.

Sargon and his immediate successors then expanded eastward and westward beyond the plains. They moved into Elam, in southern Iran, sacking many cities and at the same time raising the minor Elamite city of Susa to the status of a regional capital. In the west, the Sargonid dynasty conquered the large, powerful city-states of Mari, on the upper Euphrates; Ebla, in Syria less than fifty miles from the Mediterranean coast; and may even have temporarily occupied the hills of eastern Anatolia, a hundred miles west of the northernmost section of the Euphrates.

The Sargonids' conquests were successful because they managed to apply on a large and ambitious scale the military weapons and methods that had long been used on a small scale in Sumer and neighboring areas. Dr. Watkins here describes a Sumerian battle formation of the era of Akkad's ascendancy (mid–third millenium B.C.), as carved on the famous stone Vulture Stele (a stone marker that takes its name from its depiction of enemy dead being picked at by vultures):

> The battle-scene shows the army at the moment of victory, marching over the bodies of their defeated and slain enemies. In the upper register [band of carved figures] a troop of heavy infantry is led by the king himself; in the lower register the king is shown riding in his battle-wagon in the van [fore-

front] of a troop of light infantry. The light infantry wear no protective armor and carry no shields; each holds a long spear in the left hand and a battle-ax in the right. The heavy infantry is depicted schematically . . . [as] massed ranks of helmeted spearmen behind a front rank of men bearing shields. . . . What is significant is the number of spears projecting between the shields. The artist emphasizes the solidity of the formation, protected from chin to ankle by almost interlocking shields. The implied battle tactics anticipate those of the [Greek] Macedonian phalanx and the Roman legion. . . . It also suggests that the armies of those [Mesopotamian] city-states contained a hard core of trained professional soldiery. No seasonal levy of [local farmers]

could have managed such precision and solidarity and these soldiers were trained, uniformed and equipped to fight as a corps.[21]

The "battle-wagons" depicted on the stele, the precursors of war chariots, were clumsy, solid-wheeled carts pulled by four donkeys or onagers (wild Asiatic asses; horses were not yet widely used in the Near East). The way these vehicles were deployed in war is uncertain. But their excessive weight and inability (or poor ability at best) to pivot would have made them relatively ineffective in pitched battle; so they were probably used as "prestige" vehicles for chauffeuring the king and his officers to and from the battlefield.

Much more effective were the standard weapons of the day—the heavy spear, used

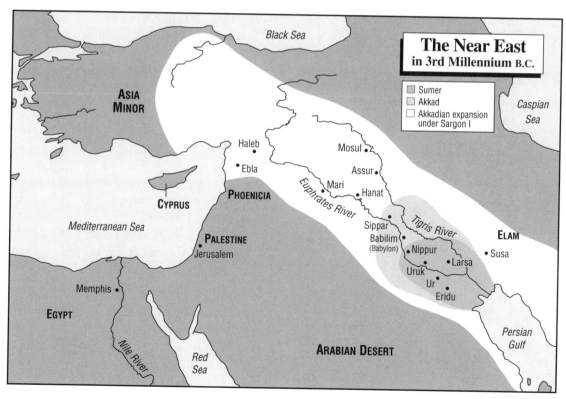

mainly for thrusting and stabbing rather than for throwing; the battle-ax, for slashing through helmets and skulls; and the dagger, used as a backup weapon. Apparently only rarely used at this time was the bow and arrow, a weapon whose effectiveness in battle would not be fully realized until centuries later. No stelae have thus far been found depicting siege warfare among the Sumerians and Akkadians, but the fact that most of the Mesopotamian cities had strong defensive walls suggests that they at least occasionally underwent direct assault. Perhaps this is where bows

A solid bronze bust of the great conqueror Sargon I, dated to ca. 2400 B.C. The eyes, which were inlaid with precious stones, were long ago removed by thieves.

came into play, with the defenders on the walls showering arrows down on attackers.

The Dream of a Unified Mesopotamia

Sargon and his heirs must have mastered all of these weapons and methods; however, they did not have a monopoly on them. Weakened by wars with neighboring peoples who had their own strong armies (and undoubtedly by other factors unknown), shortly after 2200 B.C. the Akkadian realm suddenly collapsed. And the next few centuries witnessed ongoing struggles for control of the river plains among various peoples, including Elamites, Guti (hill people from the region north of Elam), Amorites (from western Mesopotamia), and a few surviving Sumerian cities.

Though relatively short-lived, the Sargonids' domination of Mesopotamia had momentous long-term consequences, chiefly the model they set for later would-be conquerors and imperialists. As Professor Roux puts it:

> To reconstruct the unity of Mesopotamia, to reach what we would call its natural limits, became the dream of all subsequent monarchs, and from the middle of the third millennium B.C. until the fall of Babylon in 539 B.C. the history of ancient Iraq consists of their attempts, their successes, and their failures to achieve this aim.[22]

Indeed, Sargon's achievements as an empire builder would later inspire the greatest of Assyria's royal dynasties to adopt both his name and aims, with brutal but spectacular success.

2 A Duty to Conquer and Rule: The Rise of the Assyrian Nation

Among the central and northern Mesopotamian cities briefly subdued and united during the Sargonid domination of the Tigris-Euphrates region were the towns of the Assyrian homeland. This small region—which would remain the heartland of a series of Assyrian empires for more than a millennium—was centered on the upper reaches of the Tigris, where two of that river's main tributaries, the Upper and Lower Zab Rivers, flow in from the northeast. Assur, the earliest important town, named after the local patron god, was situated on the western bank of the Tigris about twenty-five miles north of the Lower Zab. Kalhu (Nimrud), Mosul, and Ninua (later Nineveh) were located on the Tigris north of its junction with the Upper Zab. "Being a highland region," the late, great Near Eastern scholar James Henry Breasted wrote:

> Assur enjoyed a climate much more invigorating than that of the hot Babylonian plain. It had many fertile valleys winding up into the eastern and northern mountains. . . . These eastern valleys were green with rolling pastures and billowing fields of barley and wheat. Herds of cattle and flocks of sheep and goats dotted the hillsides. Donkeys served as the chief draft animals, and the horse, while not unknown, was not common

in the beginning. Here flourished [Assyria's] agricultural population.[23]

At least by the era of the Akkadian conquests, the inhabitants of this north-central Mesopotamian region had acquired their own local identity, based in large degree on their worship of Assur and the religious and social customs accompanying that worship.[24]

Long of little political or military importance, Assyria began to carve out a niche in greater Mesopotamian affairs when it became an independent nation for the first time following the decline of Sumer and Akkad at the close of the third millennium B.C. For a little more than two centuries, a series of vigorous Assyrian rulers built religious temples and other public buildings, amassing power and prestige; and a few launched military campaigns into neighboring regions (too small-scale and short-lived to be called conquests—most are better described as raiding parties). In time, however, the Assyrians lost their independence, falling under the sway of various foreigners, as the main centers of power shifted, ebbed, and flowed across the Near East.

Then, in the fourteenth century B.C., Assyria experienced a new burst of national energy. This time it was as a major power,

These stylized gypsum statuettes show a man and woman grasping libation cups, then commonly used in religious ceremonies.

with aggressive kings who began a tradition of yearly military raids and conquests. These leaders, of what some modern scholars refer to as the First Assyrian Empire, set a pattern of imperial expansion and contraction that their successors would follow for centuries. According to Professor Oppenheim:

> By means of institutionalized annual campaigns, the Assyrian kings . . . succeeded in building a series of more or less ephemeral [impermanent] empires. These often collapsed suddenly—usually at the death of the king—but were again and again reconquered, to be enlarged and more carefully organized. . . . There seems to have existed within a small circle of Assyrians, particularly the natives of the town of Assur, the intense conviction that it was

their duty to reimpose the lost coherence [unity], to increase its effectiveness, and to enlarge its basis.[25]

Thus, through this curious single-minded belief—that it was their *duty* to conquer and rule—the concepts of war and expansion became deeply ingrained in the Assyrians' national character.

Assur's First Great Dynasty

Assyria first became independent at the beginning of what modern scholars call the Old Babylonian Period, lasting from about 2000 to 1600 B.C. This was overall a time of disunity and uncertainty in Near Eastern political development. Many city-states and kingdoms across Mesopotamia, like Assyria, asserted their independence, and these small states frequently engaged in disputes and wars among themselves or with various peoples living in the highland regions surrounding the plains. Occasionally, one or another of these states would suddenly burst from its home area, annex several of its neighbors, and enjoy a brief moment of expanded power and prestige. Then, beset by internal instability and external enemies, it would just as suddenly fall back to its former status or, worse, become the dependent vassal of an aggressive neighbor.

So it was with Assyria under its first powerful royal dynasty, a family of rulers fathered by King Shamshi-Adad (reigned 1813–1781 B.C.). Because a number of letters written among these rulers have been found, they are the first Assyrian monarchs about whom any personal, political, and military details are known.[26] As one of these letters attests, Shamshi-Adad first consolidated his power and prestige in Assur by building an imposing temple to the old Sumerian god, Enlil, whom, he claimed, had blessed his ascension to the throne:

> Shamshi-Adad, king of the whole world, who built the temple of the god Assur . . . he whose name the gods Anum and Enlil uttered out of regard for [his] great deeds. . . . The temple of Enlil my lord, an awesome chapel, a mighty building, the seat of my lord Enlil, that stands securely built by the work of the builders, did I build in my city Assur. To the temple I gave a roof of cedar-logs. In the chambers I set up doors of cedar wood with inlays of silver and gold . . . and I sprinkled the foundation with cedar oil, oil of the best kind, honey and butter.[27]

In time, Shamshi-Adad led his troops outward in raids and expeditions, thereby expanding Assyrian territory. He conquered the small kingdom of Mari (about 140 miles southwest of Assur), which, like Assyria, had gained its independence after the decline of Sumer and Akkad. The king installed his son, Jamsah-Adad, as ruler of Mari; then he attacked and subdued the city-state of Ekallatum, on the Tigris south of Assur, putting another son, Ishme-Dagan in charge there.

Shamshi-Adad also attempted expansion westward and southeastward. On one expedition, he marched all the way to what is now Lebanon, on the Mediterranean coast, an area from which Assyria and other Mesopotamian states imported fine cedar wood for various construction projects. He received tribute (payment acknowledging submission) from the local princes and before leaving erected a stele (stone marker) commemorating his ad-venture: "My great name and my memorial stele I set up in the country of Laban [Lebanon], on the shore of the Great Sea."[28] In the southeast, the king and his sons remained locked in almost constant warfare with the state of Eshnunna, about 160 miles from Assur, which controlled the valley of the Diyala River, another major tributary of the Tigris. With the rulers of Babylon, on the right bank of the Euphrates some two hundred miles south of Assur, Shamshi-Adad maintained a polite but cool and uneasy peace. Meanwhile, he and his sons continued to wage small-scale wars with their neighbors, constantly attempting to gain new territory, as revealed by numerous excerpts from their letters:

> Say to Jamsah-Adad: Thus says Shamshi-Adad your father. Having five days ago defeated the ruler of Qabra, now I have also defeated [the tribe] Ja'ilanum. I have also taken the town of Hibara. In this town I have made myself master of 300 of his [the ruler's] garrison troops and one of his sons. Rejoice!

> Say to Jamsah-Adad: Thus says Ishme-Dagan, your brother. As soon as I had taken the towns of Tarram, Hatka, and Shunham, I turned against Hurara. This town I surrounded. I caused siege towers and battering-rams to be raised against it, and in the course of seven days I made myself master of it. Rejoice![29]

Babylonian Interlude

Assyria's fortunes began to wane when Shamshi-Adad died in 1781 B.C. A letter marking the occasion, written by Ishme-Dagan, who succeeded him, gives the impression of a smooth transition and a still strong nation:

> Say to Jamsah-Adad: Thus says Ishme-Dagan, your brother. I have ascended the throne of my father's house. This is why I have been extremely busy, and have not been able to send you news of my well-being. . . . You must not be anxious. Your throne is and will remain your throne. The gods Adad and Shamash I hold in my hand. The peoples from Elam and the man [the king] of Eshnunna I lead by the reins. . . . Let us swear a binding oath to each other . . . [and] maintain brotherly relationships with each other for all time.[30]

Yet shortly after this correspondence, a disgruntled member of the former royal house of Mari, one Zimrilim, overthrew Jamsah-Adad and reestablished that city's independence. Both Zimrilim's and Mari's days were numbered, however; for only a few years later, in about 1759 B.C., his friend Hammurabi, king of Babylon, having recently launched his own campaign of expansion, turned on him. Mari, then the greatest metropolis of the western Euphrates plain, was destroyed forever. And soon afterward Assur and the other Assyrian cities fell under the Babylonian yoke. Within a few more years, Hammurabi had become the first ruler since Sargon to achieve the glorious dream of a united Mesopotamia. The exact extent of his kingdom remains uncertain, but it likely stretched from the Persian Gulf in the southeast to the borders of Syria and the Armenian foothills in the northwest.

Royal Sibling Squabbles

This eighteenth-century B.C. letter (quoted from Jorgen Laessoe's People of Ancient Assyria: Their Inscriptions and Correspondence*), sent by one of Shamshi-Adad's sons to a brother, attests that petty rivalries among siblings are as old as humanity.*

"Say to Ishme-Dagan: Thus says Ishhi-Adad, your brother. This is a matter that should not be discussed. And yet, let me now discuss it, so that I can let my heart breathe freely. You are a great king! You indicated to me your wish to procure two horses and I sent them to you. And now you have sent me 20 minas of tin! Have you not had your desire fulfilled by me without any discussion and in full measure?—and now you have sent me this scrap of tin! . . . What will the man say who hears this? Surely he will be unable to regard us as being on an equal footing. This house of mine is your house. What is the matter with your house that the one brother cannot grant the other brother his wish? Had you not sent me that tin, my heart certainly would not have been sick on that account. You are no great king. Why have you done this?"

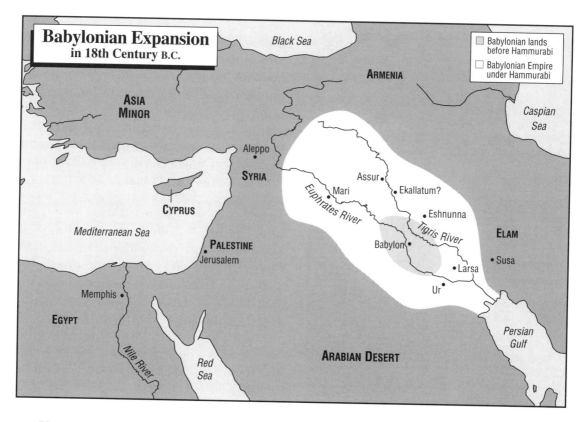

Babylonian Expansion
in 18th Century B.C.

- Babylonian lands before Hammurabi
- Babylonian Empire under Hammurabi

Black Sea

ARMENIA

ASIA MINOR

Caspian Sea

Aleppo

SYRIA

Assur · · Ekallatum?

Mari

Euphrates River

CYPRUS

Eshnunna

Tigris River

ELAM

Mediterranean Sea

PALESTINE

Jerusalem

Babylon

Susa

Larsa

Ur

Memphis

EGYPT

Persian Gulf

Nile River

ARABIAN DESERT

Red Sea

Hammurabi's successful conquests probably came a century or so too early to take full advantage of three major new military innovations that were at the time slowly but steadily taking hold in the Near East. The first of these was the widespread domestication of the horse, which was more often harnessed to chariots than ridden; the second was the perfection of woodworking techniques that allowed the construction of spoked wheels and the manufacture of lightweight chariot bodies; and the third was a new and deadlier version of a weapon already known—the composite bow (made by gluing strips of bone or sinew into grooved wood). Professor Watkins comments:

The effective development of the practical composite bow introduced a rapid fire missile delivery system necessary for mounting on the fast new chariots. . . . The composite bow gives a higher [arrow] velocity than the simple longbow, is much shorter (and therefore much easier to use, for example, in a chariot), and is capable of being kept strung for long periods without distortion or loss of power.[31]

The combination of this weapon with a fast, maneuverable firing platform—the war chariot—must have revolutionized warfare, as a massed chariotry charge, if used wisely on a relatively flat battlefield, could break and scatter an infantry formation.

Even without large contingents of horse-drawn chariotry, Hammurabi's army demonstrated sufficient military strength to enforce his rule over the cities of the

On a tablet dating from about 1750 B.C., the sun god, Shamash, bestows on Hammurabi the code of laws for which that Babylonian king later became famous.

people. Cultural ideas had traditionally flowed into Assyria from southeastern Mesopotamia, and now that Babylon had become the heir to and repository of Sumerian culture, certain influential factions of Assyrian society felt comfortable continuing this trend. As Professor Oppenheim points out, "There were circles in Assyria which looked toward Babylonia for an example and for the formation of a self-image."[32] Balancing this attitude was a strong anti-Babylonian faction that kept alive native traditions and feelings of patriotism and nationalism. Even much later, when Assyria became the dominant power in the Near East, it often looked on Babylonia as a more mature and cultivated cultural model. This love-hate relationship between Assyria and Babylonia was comparable to the later one between Rome and Greece; in each case, a nation of warriors borrowed much of its religious, literary, and other cultural ideas from the weaker but more refined neighbor it had conquered.

The Near East Increasingly Fragmented

Assyria was not the only Babylonian vassal state that resented having to do Hammurabi's bidding. This became devastatingly clear after Hammurabi's death in about 1750 B.C. Just as Shamshi-Adad's realm had disintegrated soon after his demise, Hammurabi's empire now began to crumble in the wake of numerous rebellions by the peoples he had conquered. At the same time, both old and new peoples were on the move in the Near East. During the heydays of Shamshi-Adad and Ham-

plains. Most local ruling houses, including that of Assur, became Babylonian vassals, allowed to remain in control of their own affairs as long as they did the bidding of the "Mighty King, King of Babylon, King of Sumer and Akkad, King of the Four Quarters of the World," as Hammurabi called himself. Naturally, most Assyrians deeply resented foreign political domination.

Yet Assyrian-Babylonian relations were not strictly political. The Assyrians, who were always open to foreign cultural ideas, now found themselves in a quandary, an emotional conflict concerning their Babylonian rivals that would persist throughout the remainder of their existence as a murabi, the inhabitants of central Anatolia had established a powerful military state—Hatti, centered around the city of Hattusas near the Halys River. These so-called Hit- tites began raiding southward and for a short time enjoyed considerable success, their campaigns culminating in the sack of Babylon, circa 1600 B.C.

Hammurabi's Code

The Babylonian ruler Hammurabi, who annexed Assyria in the eighteenth century B.C., *was perhaps most famous for his code of laws (based on earlier Sumerian and Akkadian regulations), which influenced the justice systems of many later Mesopotamian peoples. Here (quoted in Nels M. Bailkey's* Readings in Ancient History) *are a few of the code's 282 known laws:*

"1. If a man brings an accusation against another man, charging him with murder, but cannot prove it, the accuser shall be put to death. . . .

5. If a judge pronounce a judgment, render a decision, [or] deliver a verdict duly signed and sealed, and afterward alter his judgment, they shall call that judge to account . . . and he shall pay twelve-fold the penalty in that judgment. . . .

22. If a man practices robbery and is captured, that man shall be put to death.

23. If the robber is not captured, the man who has been robbed shall, in the presence of god, make an itemized statement of his loss, and the city and the governor in whose province . . . the robbery was committed shall compensate him for whatever he has lost. . . .

55. If a man opens his canal for irrigation and neglects it and the water carries away an adjacent field, he shall pay out grain on the basis of the adjacent field. . . .

109. If bad characters gather in the house of a wine seller and she does not arrest those bad characters and bring them to the palace, that wine seller shall be put to death. . . .

195. If a son strikes his father, they shall cut off his hand.

196. If a man destroys the eye of another man, they shall destroy his eye. . . .

229. If a builder builds a house for a man and does not make its construction sound, and the house he has built collapses and causes the death of the owner . . . that builder shall be put to death."

Quite unexpectedly, however, the Hittites quickly withdrew back into Anatolia without consolidating their gains; and the power vacuum they left behind was just as quickly filled by other peoples. The Kassites, crude and warlike highlanders from the Zagros range, east of Mesopotamia and north of Elam, now swept onto the plain and occupied Babylon. Even more impressed and influenced by Babylonian culture than the Assyrians, within only two or three generations, the Kassites had become completely absorbed and "Babylonianized," going so far as to give up their native language in favor of the Akkadian dialect spoken in Babylon.

Meanwhile, Assyria found itself caught in the middle of the ongoing struggles that increasingly fragmented the Near East into numerous small but formidable empires.

To the southeast was Kassite-controlled Babylonia, which maintained the Assyrians as vassals for a while; to the northwest and west were the Hittites, who expanded southward from Anatolia again, this time occupying Syria; and to the southwest, the Egyptians suddenly burst out of their own homeland and took control of Palestine, bringing them face-to-face with the Hittites. Complicating matters, another ambitious people, the Hurrians, set up a short-lived but very powerful state centered on the upper reaches of the Tigris. Little is known about this kingdom, called Mitanni, or its capital of Washukanni, located about two hundred miles northwest of Assur; what is certain is that in the fifteenth century B.C., Assyria fell under its sway and paid vassal allegiance to the Mitannian warlords. In this chaotic period,

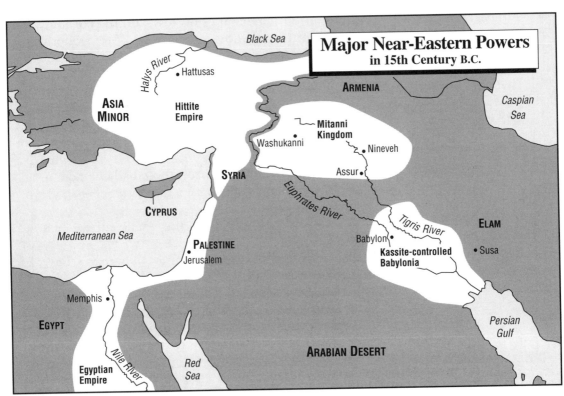

Major Near-Eastern Powers
in 15th Century B.C.

Black Sea

Halys River

• Hattusas

ARMENIA

Caspian Sea

ASIA MINOR

Hittite Empire

Mitanni Kingdom

Washukanni •

• Nineveh

SYRIA

Assur •

CYPRUS

Euphrates River

Tigris River

ELAM

Mediterranean Sea

Babylon •

• Susa

PALESTINE
Jerusalem

Kassite-controlled Babylonia

Memphis •

Persian Gulf

EGYPT

ARABIAN DESERT

Red Sea

Nile River

Egyptian Empire

which historians sometimes refer to as the "first Mesopotamian dark age," the local rulers of Assur and other Assyrian cities remain for us mere names mentioned in passing on ancient tablets. Almost nothing for certain is known about their own or their homeland's fortunes from about 1600 to the late 1300s B.C.

The First Great Period of Expansion

The darkness (in the sense both of the scarcity of surviving records and of Assyria's domination by foreigners) was suddenly lifted about 1360 B.C. A combination of increasing pressure by the Hittites in the north and civil war among Mitanni's own rulers caused the collapse of the Mitannian kingdom, leaving Assyria independent once more. The Assyrian kings now began their first great period of empire and expansion, beginning with Assuruballit I (ca. 1365–1330 B.C.), who seized large sections of former Mitannian territory.

From this time on, Assyria's foreign and military policy operated on three major fronts. The first consisted of the broad arc of foothills, ranging from the border of Hatti in the northwest, eastward through Armenia to the Zagros Mountains. The Assyrians conducted frequent small-scale raids into these northern hills, taking human captives, horses, and other booty. They also built fortresses and roads with which to defend this frontier against periodic incursions by various aggressive peoples. One large-scale campaign, conducted by Shalmaneser I (ca. 1274–1245 B.C.), resulted in the decisive defeats of an army of Armenian tribesmen and a coalition of en-

emy forces that included large contingents of Hittite mercenaries. According to one of Shalmaneser's inscriptions:

> Shattuara, king of Hani, [and] the army of Hittites and Ahlamu with him, I surrounded. He cut off the passes and my water supply. Because of thirst and fatigue my army bravely advanced into the masses of their troops, and I fought a battle and accomplished their defeat. I killed countless numbers. . . . I cut down their hordes, [and] 14,400 of them I overthrew and took as living captives. Nine of his strongholds [and] his capital city I captured. . . . The army of Hittites and Ahlami, his allies, I slaughtered like sheep.[33]

Assyria's second major front was the ever-changing border with Babylonia in the southeast. Numerous confrontations between the two powers culminated in the capture of Babylon by the vigorous Assyrian monarch Tukulti-Ninurta I (ca. 1244–1208 B.C.) some time early in his reign. In an inscription he brags:

> Trusting in Assur, Enlil, and Shamash, the great gods . . . who went at the head of my army, I forced Kashtilash, king of Babylonia, to give battle; I brought about the defeat of his armies . . . and captured Kashtilash, the Kassite king. His royal neck I trod on with my feet, like a footstool. Stripped and bound, before Assur my lord, I brought him. Sumer and Akkad to its farthest border, I brought under my sway.[34]

Despite the Assyrians' victory over their long-time rival, which naturally filled them with tremendous pride, they managed to hold on to Babylon and its southern territories for only a short time. The Kassite-Babylonian nobles soon rebelled and regained control of their city; and not long after that, in about 1160 B.C., a strong Elamite king took Babylon, eradicating the Kassite line of rulers for good and carrying the most sacred statue of the god Marduk back to Susa in triumph.

On its third major military front, the western corridor to Syria and the Mediterranean Sea, Assyria launched relentless offensives. Gaining, losing, and then regaining territory in cycles, they at first took advantage of the fact that the Hittites and Egyptians were at each other's throats over possession of Palestine and Syria. This rivalry reached its climax in a bloody clash at Kadesh (or Qadesh, in southern Syria), in about 1285 B.C., one of the greatest battles fought in ancient times. The outcome was indecisive, however; and sixteen years later these enemies signed a treaty, probably because they both now feared Assyria's growing power. And they had good reason to fear. The Assyrian king Adad-Nirari I (ca. 1305–1274 B.C.) reached Carchemish, in northern Syria, less than ninety miles from the sea, as did his immediate successor, Shalmaneser. These and later Assyrian conquests posed an almost constant threat, not only to major powers like Egypt and Hatti, but also to the stability of the many small kingdoms in the region, including the early Jewish states of Israel and Judah.

Sudden Catastrophe

As it turned out, however, when the complicated balance of power in the area was suddenly overturned circa 1200 B.C., the aggressive Assyrians were not the culprits. At about that time, the northern and western parts of the Near East, as well as large areas of the Mediterranean world beyond, underwent an unexpected and catastrophic upheaval of unprecedented scope. Throughout this region, almost all of the leading towns and cities were sacked, burned, and destroyed, most never to be rebuilt; among them were Hattusas and the other important Hittite centers, bringing about Hatti's sudden and utter collapse; Ugarit and other prosperous Syrian and Palestinian coastal ports were plundered and devastated; in the distant northwest, Mycenae and the other Bronze Age kingdoms of Greece met a similar fate; and at the same time Egypt came under direct assault by maritime hordes they called the "sea peoples," whom the Egyptians barely managed to beat back, at great personal costs.

Historians have advanced a number of theories to explain this widespread catastrophe. Some think that rapid local population growth among the semibarbarous tribes inhabiting "Eurasia," the vast steppe lands north of the Black and Caspian Seas, caused them to migrate southward in search of new lands, destroying all in their path. Others suggest that climatic factors, such as a prolonged dry spell, caused these mass migrations. Another theory discounts the idea of mass migrations; it holds instead that a large portion of the destruction was caused by civil conflicts, economic collapse, and other crises within the Near Eastern states themselves, which less civilized peoples on the periphery then took advantage of. And still another view, advanced recently by Robert Drews of Vanderbilt University, is that military innovations among these "periphery" peoples suddenly gave their foot soldiers the ability to defeat the

A horde of unknown "barbarians" attacks the northern fringes of Assyrian territory. Somehow Assyria managed to survive the devastating upheavals that erased Hatti from the map and overthrew many of the most powerful cities of the western Near East in about 1200 B.C.

chariot corps that had for centuries been the mainstay of Near Eastern armies.[35]

Whatever the causes of these disasters, as Drews says, "Assur and the other cities of the Assyrian heartland came through the catastrophe unscathed."[36] Perhaps the location of the Assyrian heartland, hundreds of miles inland from the main zone of destruction, kept it safe. In any case, with Hatti erased from the map, Palestine in disarray, and Egypt temporarily weakened from its bout with the sea peoples, Assyria was now the lone surviving great power in the western Near Eastern sphere. In truth, this distinction was not as great as it sounds; for the confusions and dislocations accompanying the catastrophe had led to

the sudden rise in power and influence of several formerly insignificant local peoples. Among these were the Aramaeans, tribal inhabitants of the Syrian deserts, who now presented a partial barrier to Assyrian expansion. Professor Roux explains:

The vacuum created in Syria by the collapse of the Hittite empire . . . encouraged the Aramaeans to invade the Syrian hinterland, to cross the Euphrates, and to penetrate deeper and deeper into Mesopotamia, settling as they advanced and forming . . . a network of kingdoms, large or small, which enclosed Assur and Babylon in an ever-narrowing circle.[37]

Strong evidence of the Aramaeans' steadily growing influence was the fact that their language, Aramaic (a Semitic tongue that used a relatively simple alphabet rather than clumsy cuneiform), spread far and wide, eventually competing with Akkadian in Assyria and later, after Assyria's fall, becoming the universal language of the entire Near East.

Vanquishing the Enemies of Assur

Despite the obstacles to expansion presented by the Aramaeans and other newly ascendant peoples, the Assyrian kings, whose yearly military forays continued unabated, occasionally enjoyed some considerable success. The most outstanding gains made in this period were those of Tiglath-pileser I (ca. 1115–1077 B.C.), who expanded the realm on all three of its major fronts.[38] He began on the northern front, first vanquishing an invasion of Anatolian tribesmen, the Mushki, who threatened Nineveh, and then subduing other aggressive tribes deep in the hills of Armenia north of Lake Van. On the western front, he marched against the Aramaeans, pushing them back from the Euphrates and taking some of their strongholds. On this campaign, he managed to fulfill the long-held Assyrian dream of reaching the Mediterranean coast (accomplished briefly by Shamshi-Adad seven centuries before), where he received tribute from Byblos, Sidon, and other Phoenician cities. Finally, on the southern front, Tiglathpileser

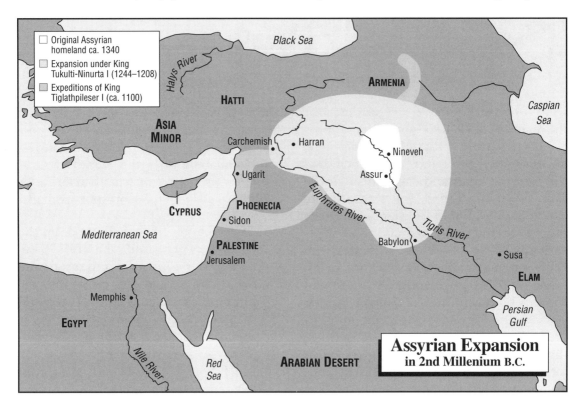

Map legend:
- Original Assyrian homeland ca. 1340
- Expansion under King Tukulti-Ninurta I (1244–1208)
- Expeditions of King Tiglathpileser I (ca. 1100)

Assyrian Expansion in 2nd Millenium B.C.

A carved relief from the palace at Nineveh shows the forces of King Tiglathpileser I storming an enemy town. The bodies of enemy prisoners hang on stakes (at upper left).

gained tremendous prestige by capturing Babylon; apparently he did not gain much else from this foray, however, for he did not follow up with further conquests of Babylonian territory.

Tiglathpileser successfully extended Assyria's borders to their greatest extent to date. And thereby he fulfilled what he and his predecessors believed was their duty to their gods—to conquer and expand. Among the surviving records of his reign, one text proclaims:

> Assur and the great gods, who have made my kingdom great, and who have bestowed might and power as a gift, commanded that I should extend the boundary of their land, and they entrusted to my hand their mighty weapons, the storm of battle. Lands, mountains, cities, and princes, the enemies of Assur, I have brought under my

sway, and have subdued their territories. . . . Unto Assyria I added land, unto her peoples, peoples. I enlarged the frontier of my land, and all their lands I brought under my sway.[39]

Yet, as had happened so often in the past, these gains proved only temporary. Tiglathpileser was assassinated circa 1077 B.C., and his immediate successors, far less vigorous and capable than he, were unable to maintain the cohesion of so large a realm inhabited by so many diverse peoples. So that realm quickly shrank, shedding its conquered territories one by one until, some sixteen decades after Tiglathpileser's death, all that remained was the core—the traditional Assyrian heartland centered around Assur and Nineveh.

These decades, about which little is known, constitute a second Mesopotamian dark age. Available evidence suggests that during these years the Near East was plagued by small-scale civil discords, as well as floods, famines, and widespread poverty and hardship. On the political front, with Assyria and Babylonia quiescent, the Aramaeans and other seminomadic peoples were able to make periodic gains. No doubt they thought Assyria's days as a great power were over and that they would soon whittle away and overwhelm its last vestiges. They had no way of knowing that, unlike Sumer, Mitanni, Hatti, and so many other once-great Mesopotamian realms, Assyria had not sunk forever into oblivion. To the contrary, the masters of Assur were about to enjoy a rebirth of nationalism and imperialism that would profoundly transform the Near East and strike terror into the hearts of all its peoples.

3 A Name Once More to Be Dreaded: Assyria Is Reborn

During the roughly 160 years of its second and bleakest dark age, Assyria's once considerable realm continued to shrink. And by the start of the last decade of the tenth century B.C., the nation had reached its lowest ebb of power and territory since it had first become independent over a thousand years before. It now consisted only of its original heartland, measuring barely one hundred miles long and fifty miles wide, straddling the junction of the Tigris and Upper Zab. But the Assyrians had lost more than just the lands they had conquered in the days of Tiglathpileser and his predecessors. They had also lost access to the vital trade routes running through the steppe lands in the west and mountain passes in the north; and this meant that economic collapse was, sooner or later, inevitable.

Yet despite these adversities, Assyria possessed certain important advantages that, if properly exploited, might realize an immense hidden potential. Its principal cities were still free; its warriors, superbly trained by year after year of hard campaigning, were the toughest and fiercest in the known world; and its ruling dynasty was still intact after more than two centuries, its members keeping alive the promise of reviving the glories of their ancestors. Beginning with Adad-Nirari II (ca. 911–891 B.C.),

a series of strong kings kept that promise, transforming Assyria into the largest, most feared empire the world had yet seen.

It would be misleading, however, to describe this great empire as a systematic, organized enterprise in which each king followed an overriding plan of expansion and addition of new provinces to administer. Although the Assyrian kings had the same overall aims—namely to wage war and conquer—these goals were usually more short termed and narrowly defined. As Professor Roux points out:

> The wars which the Assyrian monarchs waged year after year . . . had three different, though closely interwoven motives. . . . They were fundamentally defensive, or rather preventive wars aiming at protecting "the land of the god Assur" from its hostile neighbors. Then since a victorious campaign meant the capture of men and booty, and since a vanquished country could be persuaded to pay regular tribute, they were predatory wars. . . . As long as foreign countries could be plundered and were willing to pay the ransom of their independence, there was no need to annex and govern them. Last but not least, there was behind these armed expeditions a religious, almost a moral motive. . . . The king's enemies

were the god's enemies; they were "wicked devils deserving punisment."[40]

Thus, each campaign was partly self-defense, partly piracy, and partly a religious crusade; and as a crusade undertaken in the god's name, any means used to achieve success, no matter how harsh or brutal, were seen as justifiable. This was the basis for the systematic cruelty for which the Assyrians became infamous. "The crack of the whip," Nahum the Hebrew later recalled, "and the rumble of the

The five rows of relief on this black obelisk commemorating the victories of King Shalamaneser III depict vanquished peoples offering him tribute. Among these defeated enemies is Jehu, king of Israel.

wheel, galloping horse and bounding chariot! . . . Hosts of the slain, heaps of corpses, dead bodies without end—they stumble over the bodies!"[41]

An Empire Out of Necessity

Indeed, consistently aggressive, pitiless, and often savage tactics and policies characterized all of the leaders of the new Assyria, including Adad-Nirari II, who initiated the nation's sudden rebirth. "Powerful in battle, who overthrows cities, who burns the mountains of the lands, am I," he stated.

> Strong hero, who consumes his enemies, who burns up the wicked and the evil, am I. . . . Like the onset of a storm, I press on. Like an evil downpour, I rage. . . . Like a net, I entangle. . . . At the mention of my mighty name, the princes of the four regions (of the world) trembled.[42]

This propaganda, designed to impress and frighten adversaries, was exaggerated to say the least; Adad-Nirari certainly does not rank among the ablest and greatest of Assyria's new conquerors. Yet by driving the Aramaeans out of the Tigris valley, recapturing some of the nation's lost cities in the steppes west of the Tigris, and rebuilding some old and ruined cities, he unknowingly opened the final and most glorious chapter in Assyria's long history. He bragged:

> The defeat of the desert folk, the Aramaeans, was accomplished. . . . I am he who returned the cities Hit, Idu, and Zakku, strongholds of Assyria, to the territory of this land. . . . The old city

of Apku, which the kings who went before me had built, had fallen [in]to decay and was turned to a mound of ruins. That city I rebuilt. . . . I made it beautiful, I made it splendid, I made it greater than it had been before.[43]

Adad-Nirari's successors consistently adopted this theme of "greater than before," each attempting to glorify himself and the god Assur through military deeds and building programs (either new buildings or restorations of old ones). His son, Tukulti-Ninurta II (ca. 890–884 B.C.), for example, both consolidated his gains and refurbished Assur's defensive walls. As each new king launched his nearly yearly raiding parties and small-scale campaigns, a little more territory and a few new towns came under Assyrian domination. At first, as had long been the custom, most of the conquered towns and peoples kept their native rulers, who were vassals to Assyria's king; but the larger the realm grew, the more difficult it became to collect tribute from and suppress rebellions in distant areas. It therefore became more expedient to make many of these areas official provinces, each ruled by an Assyrian governor appointed by the king in Assur. Thus, a true empire with complex administrative machinery gradually grew out of necessity, but always on a piecemeal basis.

The economic system Assyria imposed on its provinces was straightforward, self-centered, and severe. Foodstuffs, livestock, precious metals, and other commodities and riches regularly flowed into the empire's heartland from outlying areas; but very little, if anything, flowed out to compensate people for their losses. "The Assyrians took much and gave very little," Roux points out, "with the result that if the state was rich, its distant subjects were destitute

and in almost constant rebellion."[44] To guard against such insurrections and generally keep local populations in line, the state maintained networks of spies and garrisons of soldiers in each subordinate area and with these vigorously enforced obedience. When individuals or groups proved continually unruly, Assyrian leaders sometimes killed them, but more often simply uprooted and moved them. Daniel Snell comments:

> Like some earlier Mesopotamian imperialists, [the Assyrians] practiced deportation, resettling [people] in other places, frequently in the heartland of Assyria itself. Perhaps 4.5 million persons were deported over three centuries, most in the period from 745 to 627 B.C. This kind of exile was intended to destroy the person's individuality and rebelliousness, and it seems to have usually worked in the short run.[45]

A Ruler Not to Be Trifled With

Using these and other harsh and ruthless methods, the first great monarch of the new empire, Assurnasirpal II (ca. 883–859 B.C.), Tukulti-Ninurta's son, made Assyria once more a name to be dreaded in the Near East. After consolidating his father's gains, in about 877 B.C. the new king boldly marched his forces westward, hoping to do what no other Assyrian monarch had done since the mighty Tiglathpileser more than two centuries before—reach the Mediterranean shores. Assurnasirpal first fought his way through Aramaean-held territory until he reached Carchemish, on the west bank of the upper Euphrates. His detailed

Found in the ruins of the palace of Assurnasirpal II, at Nimrud, this relief shows that king marching in a procession.

annals, many of which have survived, tell how he then continued westward, covering approximately twenty miles a day, crossed the Orontes River, and finally reached the "Great Sea":

> At that time I marched along the side of Mount Lebanon, and to the Great Sea. . . . In the Great Sea I washed my weapons, and I made offerings unto the gods. The tribute of the kings of the seacoast, of the people of Tyre, Sidon, Byblos, Mahalata . . . silver, gold, lead, copper, vessels of copper, garments made of brightly colored wool . . . maple-wood, boxwood, and ivory . . . I received as tribute from them, and they embraced my feet. . . . I made offerings to the gods, and I fashioned a memorial stele of my valor, and there I set it up.[46]

Soon afterward, Assurnasirpal headed home. Since he did not leave an army behind to enforce his rule over the coastal peoples, the expedition proved to be less a conquest and more a large-scale raid for plunder. Yet it was also a brilliant show of force, demonstrating to all the peoples of the Near East that the masters of Assur could march their formidable armies over great distances and strike any and all at will. And if and when they struck, there was more to fear than mere defeat. Assurnasirpal also firmly established a reputation for terror and cruelty surpassing all of his predecessors. The annals of one campaign proudly boast:

> I captured the city; 600 of their warriors I put to the sword; 3,000 captives I burned with fire; I did not leave a single one among them alive to serve as a hostage. Hulai, their governor, I captured alive. Their corpses I formed into pillars [piles]; their young men and maidens I burned in the fire. Hulai . . . I flayed [skinned], his skin I spread upon the wall of the city . . . [and] the city I destroyed.[47]

In other annals, the king listed more atrocities, including cutting off noses, ears, fingers, and other mutilations, impaling some victims on sharp stakes, and entombing others inside palace walls. Clearly, this was not a ruler to be trifled with.

Commanders and Their Troops

The main instrument of the cruelty displayed by Assurnasirpal and his successors was, of course, the strong, well-organized,

Assurnasirpal's New Palace

Although by both ancient and modern standards Assurnasirpal was a bloodthirsty conqueror, like most other Assyrian kings he was a builder as well as destroyer. This excerpt from his annals (quoted in Daniel D. Luckenbill's Ancient Records of Assyria and Babylonia*), describes his renovations of the city of Nimrud, including the erection of a beautiful palace.*

"That city had fallen into ruins and lay prostrate. That city I built anew, and the peoples whom my hand had conquered, from the lands which I brought under my sway . . . I took and I settled them therein. The ancient mound I destroyed, and I dug down to the water level. . . . A palace of cedar, cypress, juniper, boxwood, mulberry, pistachio-wood, and tamarisk, for my royal dwelling and for my lordly pleasure for all time I founded therein. Beasts of the mountains and of the seas of white limestone and alabaster I fashioned, and set them up in its gates, I adorned it, I made it glorious, and put copper clothes-hooks all around it. Door-leaves of cedar, cypress, juniper, and mulberry I hung in the gates thereof; and silver, gold, lead, copper, and iron, the spoil of my hand from the lands which I had brought under my sway, in great quantities I took and placed therein."

and brutally efficient Assyrian army. In this early period of the new empire, that army's ranks were filled in large degree by a levy of native Assyrians, who were drafted into service at the start of a campaign and returned to their farming or other labors at the campaign's end. A branch of the civil service was devoted to keeping census records of the empire's towns and villages to facilitate quick and efficient mobilization of manpower (those called up were sometimes used on large communal projects, such as building palaces or digging canals). As more foreign peoples came under imperial control, vassal rulers were obliged to supply men for the army's auxiliary units; and some mercenaries (including Aramaeans) were also used.

The army's commander in chief was, not surprisingly, the king, who led most major military campaigns. Under him served his trusted "field marshal," or *tartanu,* responsible for implementing and overseeing the actual field operations. And under the *tartanu* stretched an efficient chain of command that included commanders of units of 1,000, 200, 100, and 50 men each, as well as leaders of "sections," groups of 10 men each, not unlike modern army platoons. Chariots were grouped into squadrons of 50, each with its own commander. These various officers communicated regularly with those above or below them via messengers. One surviving dispatch reads:

> To you have been assigned . . . 1,119 men . . . [who] are destined for the infantry of the palace. Why then are you yourself transferring some to the fully equipped soldiers [i.e., heavy infantry], others to the elite soldiers [specially trained royal troops], and still others to the cavalry, making them part of your own regiment? . . . I am now sending this message to you: "Summon them, even if many of them are elsewhere . . . [for] they all have to be present for my officer when he checks on them!" I am now sending my officer; he will muster them.[48]

The total number of troops commanded by the king, field marshal, and their commanders is uncertain and probably varied considerably from one campaign to another. A text from the Mari archives of the second millennium B.C. mentions a force of 100,000 infantry, 20,000 archers, and 1,500 cavalry (this was before the introduction of massed chariotry). These impressive numbers are probably exaggerated, although by how much it is impossible to say. Later, in the first millennium, Assurnasirpal II and some of his successors may have fielded armies that size on rare occasions; however, a typical annual campaigning force was almost certainly much smaller.

Weapons and Tactics

Some of the weapons and tactics of the new Assyrian army were similar to those used in the late second millennium B.C. The principal weapon was the bow, most often utilized in the main tactical field unit—the archer-pair. This consisted of two men, the first a spear- or dagger-man bearing a very large shield, the top of which curved up and back to form a kind of canopy to protect against incoming arrows and other missiles. Made of tightly packed bundles of wicker bound with leather, such shields were light but very sturdy. The second man, the archer, who huddled with his companion behind the shield, used a powerful composite bow to fire off volleys of arrows. Rows of hundreds or thousands of these pairs, who in battle moved forward in unison, made up the mainstay of the Assyrian infantry.

Chariots featured a similar arrangement—a driver and an archer standing behind a protective screen mounted on the vehicle's front (a third man was added later). However, by the beginning of the new Assyrian Empire, chariots had greatly diminished in number and importance in favor of an increasing use of cavalry, which at first, like the infantry, operated in two-man units. According to Robert Drews:

> The earliest representations of archers shooting from the backs of galloping horses are ninth-century B.C. Assyrian reliefs . . . [showing] the cavalry archers operating in pairs: one cavalryman holds the reins of both his own and his partner's horse, allowing the partner to use his hands for the bow and bowstring. The early cavalry teams thus parallel exactly the charioteer and chariot archer. The cavalry archer was undoubtedly less accurate than his counterpart on a chariot. . . . But in other respects the cavalry teams were surely superior. They were able, first of all, to operate in terrain too rough for wheeled vehicles.

A modern rendering of Assyrian soldiers shows the members of an archer-pair (the men at left and right) conversing with a third soldier (holding a severed head).

And their chances for flight, when things went wrong, were much better. . . . If a cavalryman's horse was killed or injured . . . [he] could immediately leap on the back of his partner's horse and so ride out of harm's way.[49]

The Assyrian army was also highly adept at the techniques of siege warfare, which they applied methodically and ferociously when enemies retreated into walled towns rather than face them in open battle. About such a stronghold, one of Assurnasirpal's annals states:

The city was exceedingly strong and was surrounded by three walls. The men [enemy soldiers] trusted in their mighty walls and in their hosts, and did not come down [into the open], and did not embrace my feet. With battle and slaughter I stormed [besieged] the city and captured it. 3,000 of their warriors I put to the sword.[50]

Noted Assyriologist D. J. Wiseman here describes some of the siege techniques used by Assurnasirpal and his successors:

A ramp or causeway of piled up earth, rubble or wood enabled the attacker to gain closer access to the upper, more penetrable . . . walls. A battering ram was brought up by animal traction and then manhandled into position. This formidable weapon was a ram of metal-

Comradeship in Arms?

Here, from his Life in the Ancient Near East, *historian Daniel Snell comments on how the way Assyrian soldiers were paid may have affected (or reflected?) relations between officers and regular troops.*

"The military was the most spectacular of the [state-controlled] schemes for labor exploitation. Probably a large part of the upkeep of the troops came directly from the towns they looted, but when there was peace or duty that did not involve pillage, troops were paid with rations from government stores. These rations were the same for both officers and men. That means that they were intended for basic upkeep while on noncombat duty, but it also shows that the army cultivated an ethic of egalitarianism [equality], like the modern Israeli army, which allowed its officers to draw on comradeship in arms as well as the power of command and coercion to get their men to do ridiculously dangerous things."

The Assyrians were famous for their prowess in siege warfare, as evidenced by this rendering of a stone relief showing a siege tower with attached battering ram. Many later peoples emulated Assyrian siege techniques.

tipped wood housed in a wooden framework shielded by a covering. It was propelled on wheels or foot to dislodge the upper brickwork [of the walls] or smash down gateways or weak places. . . . Where the objective lay by a river, the Assyrians used a siege tower. Constructed upstream and floated into position, this gave a field of fire down onto the defenders within the walls. . . . Meanwhile sappers [miners], covered by bowmen and shields, attempted to tunnel and undermine the walls.[51]

Showdown at Qarqar

Such war tactics and techniques were applied with unusual energy and relentlessness by Assurnasirpal's son, Shalamaneser III (ca. 858–824 B.C.), who devoted fully thirty-one of his reign's nearly thirty-five years to vigorous military offensives. Shalamaneser campaigned on all three of the nation's traditional fronts, leading Assyrian forces as far afield as the Persian Gulf in the south, the Zagros range in the east, and Palestine in the west; however, two factors kept him from adding much new territory to the empire. First, he tended not to follow up on his victories by imposing military and administrative structures on the conquered. For example, he enjoyed several victories in southern Armenia, where a new kingdom, Urartu, had recently risen; and also farther east, in what is now northern Iran, where he fought two other new peoples, the Medes and Persians. In both cases, Shalamaneser seemed content to sack and loot cities, receive tribute, and then withdraw, which only allowed these peoples to continue amassing power. Ironically, one of them, the Medes, would eventually play a leading role in Assyria's downfall.

The other factor frustrating Shalamaneser's efforts at expansion was that he faced much tougher opposition than his father and other ancestors, especially in the west. There, coalitions of small states frequently formed to bar his path. He encountered the most formidable of these alliances in 853 B.C. when, bent on marching to the sea, he moved his army into the plains of central Syria. The fateful showdown, at Qarqar on the Orontes River some 120 miles north of Damascus, was one of the largest battles fought anywhere in the world in the first half of the first millennium B.C. Arrayed against the Assyrians were more than seventy thousand allied troops, and Shalamaneser likely commanded comparable forces. In the course of claiming victory, one of his annals lists some specifics about his opponents:

1,200 chariots, 1,200 cavalry, 20,000 soldiers, of Hadadezer of Damascus; 700 chariots, 700 cavalry, 10,000 soldiers of Irhuleni of Hamath; 2,000 chariots, 10,000 soldiers of Ahab, the Israelite. . . . I battled with them. From Qarqar, as far as the city of Gilzau, I routed them. 14,000 of their warriors I slew with the sword. . . . I scattered their corpses far and wide. . . . In that battle I took from them their chariots, their cavalry, their horses, broken to the yoke.[52]

Boasts like this one were standard for Assyrian monarchs, regardless of whether they won or lost a fight. The truth is that Shalamaneser did not achieve victory at Qarqar; rather, the armies fought to what was essentially a draw, and the Assyrians, unable to capture Damascus, soon withdrew.

Tiglathpileser's Reforms

After this disappointment in the west, Shalamaneser faced another and darker one much closer to home. In about 827 B.C., one of his sons, Assurdaninapli, rebelled, taking charge of Assur, Nineveh, and some other important towns. Now a bitter old man, the king remained largely in seclusion in his palace at Nimrud and delegated the task of fighting the civil war to another son, Shamshi-Adad V. The conflict was still raging when Shalamaneser died in 824. Shamshi-Adad succeeded his father and soon afterward defeated the rebels, but had to spend the remainder of his reign (ca. 824–811 B.C.) reasserting authority over foreign vassals who had taken advantage of the civil war and staged their own rebellions. There then followed a period of over half a century in which Assyria remained largely stagnant due to a combination of lackluster rulers and continued internal instability.

This period of weakness and inactivity ended quite suddenly with the crowning of Tiglathpileser III (ca. 744–727 B.C.), one of Assyria's greatest monarchs and imperialists. An intelligent, energetic, and innovative ruler, Tiglathpileser correctly reasoned that the empire could not survive, let alone grow, without major administrative and military reforms; so he wasted no time in instituting them. Overall, the administrative changes were designed to increase the powers of the central authority over those of various individuals and regions, both domestic and foreign. Professor Roux explains:

> In Assyria proper the existing districts were multiplied and made smaller. Outside Assyria [foreign vassals] . . . were, whenever possible or suitable, deprived of their local rulers and transformed into provinces. Each province was treated like an Assyrian district and entrusted to a . . . "governor" (*shaknu*, literally: "appointed") responsible to the king. The countries and peoples who could not be incorporated into the empire were left with their own government but placed under the supervision of an "overseer" (*qepu*). A very efficient system of communications was established between the royal court and the provinces.[53]

In the military sphere, Tiglathpileser replaced the army, which had long been largely made up of Assyrian men conscripted on a periodic basis, with a permanent professional force consisting mostly of foreigners from the provinces. He also

A limestone bas-relief, dated to the seventh century B.C., shows the head of Tiglathpileser III, one of the most effective and successful of all Assyria's kings.

significantly increased the army's size, although the specific numbers remain unknown.

With this new army, the king marched west and attacked Syria, where he defeated a force of Aramaeans and soon afterward another force sent by the king of Urartu to aid them. One Aramaean city, Arpad, resisted, but fell after a three-year siege and became the capital of a new Assyrian province. After annexing most of Syria and probably also Phoenicia, on the Mediterranean coast, Tiglathpileser received tribute from many frightened local kings, including those of Damascus and Israel.

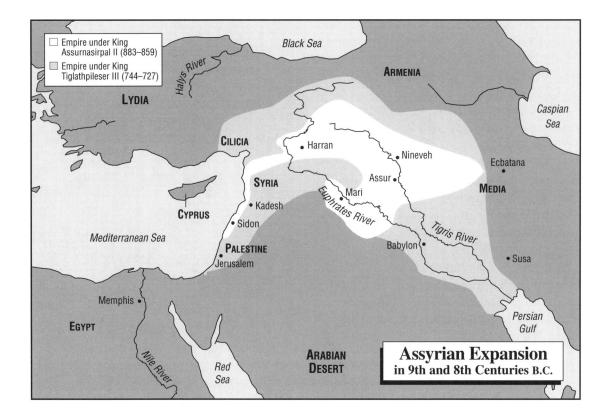

Map legend:
- Empire under King Assurnasirpal II (883–859)
- Empire under King Tiglathpileser III (744–727)

Black Sea
ARMENIA
Caspian Sea
LYDIA
Halys River
CILICIA
Harran
Nineveh
Ecbatana
SYRIA
Assur
MEDIA
Mari
CYPRUS
Kadesh
Euphrates River
Sidon
Tigris River
Mediterranean Sea
PALESTINE
Babylon
Susa
Jerusalem
Memphis
Persian Gulf
EGYPT
Nile River
ARABIAN DESERT
Red Sea

Assyrian Expansion
in 9th and 8th Centuries B.C.

Then the Assyrian army departed and marched eastward into the Zagros range to fight the Medes and other hill peoples. With Tiglathpileser's main forces gone, the rulers of Palestine suddenly grew bold and formed an anti-Assyrian coalition, which turned out to be a fatal mistake. The Assyrian king returned, crushed the rebels, and not long afterward seized Damascus and half of Israel.

In 727 B.C. Tiglathpileser died, or as many Mesopotamians then phrased it, "went to his destiny." During a reign of less than twenty years, he had managed to reinvigorate a declining realm and to set Assyria once more firmly on the path of "glorious" conquest and expansion. His successors, who would in the following century elevate the empire to its great zenith, clearly owed him an incalculable debt.

4 Sargon and His Heirs: The Assyrian Empire at Its Height

Tiglathpileser's administrative reforms had made Assyria a great empire and paved the way for that state's eventual domination of almost the entire Near East. His son, Shalamaneser V, had a very short reign (ca. 726–722 B.C.), information about which is obscure. All that is known for sure is that he died while laying siege to a Palestinian city. By contrast, a great deal is known about Shalamaneser's successor, Sargon II; in fact, the reigns of Sargon and his immediate successors—Sennacherib, Esarhaddon, and Assurbanipal, collectively referred to by historians as the Sargonids—are the best documented of any Mesopotamian rulers. German philologist and historian Wolfram von Soden briefly summarizes the nature of this rich legacy of sources:

> Each king left behind numerous and often lengthy inscriptions, which both in style and in what they say or do not say bear the stamp of the royal personality. A great body of correspondence, mostly from Nineveh and in the Assyrian and Babylonian languages, is extremely fruitful as well. . . . The Old Testament, and occasionally Greek reports, are of supplementary significance. Finally should be mentioned the pictorial accounts on the palace walls.[54]

Through these surviving records, we can with some confidence reconstruct the main events and fortunes of the Assyrian Empire under Sargon and his heirs. This vast realm, by far the largest in world history to date, controlled the entire courses of the Tigris and Euphrates Rivers, penetrated into the Zagros range in the east, Armenia (Urartu) in the north, Anatolia in the northwest, and had windows on the Persian Gulf and Mediterranean Sea. It should be stressed, however, that though very large, this empire was at all times unstable and prone to collapse. This was partly because of the difficulty of maintaining control of so many diverse lands and peoples, each with their own customs and ambitions. But contributing even more to the empire's lack of cohesion were the Assyrians' harsh and oppressive policies and tactics, which encouraged subject peoples time and again to rebel.

"The Heat of My Terrible Weapons"

For this reason, the political history of Sargon's reign (ca. 722–705 B.C.) amounts to little more than a relentless struggle against such rebellions. The circumstances of his famous eighth campaign, into Urartu, serves as a potent example. Urartu had grown increasingly strong in recent years and became a menace to Assyria, not only directly, by threatening their shared border, but also indirectly, by stirring up rebellions among nearby Assyrian vassal states. Sargon reasoned that crushing Urartu and punishing its king, Ursa (or Rusas), would discourage further rebellions in the area.

So in 714 B.C., the eighth year of his reign, the Assyrian king, attempting to live up to the name he had chosen—that of the great conqueror of old, Sargon of Akkad—led his forces northward to smite his enemy. His annals vividly capture the rugged, dangerous trek. "I directed the line of march into the mountains," he states. They were

> high mountains covered with all kinds of trees, whose surface was a jungle, whose passes were frightful, over whose area shadows stretch as in a cedar forest, the traveler of whose paths never sees the light of the sun . . . on whose sides gorges and precipices yawn, to look at which with the eyes, inspires fear; its road was too rough for chariots to mount, bad for horses, and too steep to march footsoldiers over. With [a] quick and keen understanding . . . I had my men carry mighty pickaxes . . . and they shattered the side of the high mountain . . . making a good road.[55]

Along the way, terrified at the approach of the dreaded Assyrian host, delegations from minor tribes and peoples offered submission and tribute.

Eventually, the army approached the valley in which King Ursa waited with his own forces. The only way to reach the valley was by scaling an ice-covered mountain ridge, and Sargon himself led the way, intrepidly walking and climbing while attendants carried his chariot. Once in sight of the Urartians, the Assyrians attacked at once and within a short time sent them, including King Ursa, into panicked flight. Sargon's forces then gave chase, slaughtering many stragglers, as Sargon's annals describe:

> I cut down their army and broke up their organization. I defeated the armies of Urartu, the wicked enemy, and their allies. . . . I filled the gullies and gorges with their horses while they, like ants in distress, made their way over most difficult trails. In the heat of my terrible weapons I went up after them.[56]

The great king Sargon II, founder of the Sargonid dynasty, and one of his advisers are seen on this eighth-century B.C. bas-relief found at Sargon's palace at Dur-Sharrukin (modern Khorsabad).

Afterward, rather than face certain torture and execution at Sargon's hands, Ursa committed suicide. To discourage future rebellions, Sargon mercilessly burned many towns, crops, and forests in Urartu and surrounding regions.

A New City All His Own

The north was not the only region in which Sargon found himself stamping out rebellions. Supported by Elam, still one of Assyria's archenemies, a dynasty of Chaldeans (Aramaeans living in what was once Sumer, near the Persian Gulf) seized Babylon's throne and renounced Assyrian control. Sargon marched against the Babylonians and Elamites, joining them in battle between the Tigris River and the Zagros foothills. Per the Assyrian custom, he claimed a great victory in his annals; but Babylonian texts reveal the truth—that Sargon was defeated.[57] Assyria's southward advance was temporarily checked, and the Chaldean usurper, Merodach-Baladan, remained in power for eleven years. Finally, in about 710 B.C., Sargon achieved his revenge by invading Babylonia again, and this time he was successful. Merodach-Baladan fled to Elam, and the Assyrian king entered Babylon in triumph. Sargon was also victorious against a group of Syrian rebels, as well as the king of Gaza, in southern Palestine, who had revolted with the assistance of a small Egyptian army.

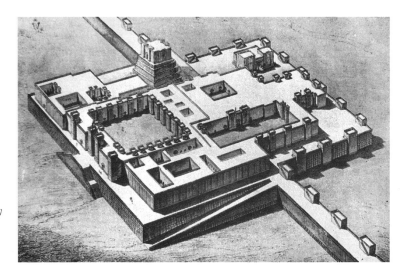

This modern restoration shows what Sargon's palace at Dur-Sharrukin probably looked like at its height of splendor and prestige in the late eighth century B.C. Incredibly, the magnificent structure was abandoned soon after it was built.

Amid these and other grueling long-distance campaigns, Sargon somehow found the time to make his mark as a great builder. At first, he resided in Nimrud, where he restored and modified the magnificent palace erected by Assurnasirpal more than a century and a half before (and which Austen Henry Layard would bring to light over twenty-five centuries later). But Sargon soon decided that he wanted to create a new palace in a new city all his own. In about 717 B.C., he laid the first foundations at Dur-Sharrukin (meaning "Sargon's fortress"), modern Khorsabad, then a virgin site about fifteen miles northeast of Nineveh. According to the noted Near Eastern scholar A. T. Olmstead:

> [Both] city and palace were the work of Tab-shar-Assur, the [realm's] chief architect. . . . The city was laid out in the form of a rough rectangle, nearly two thousand yards on a side, and was oriented with its corners approximately to the cardinal points [north, south, east, and west]. Up to the city led a roughly paved road, forty feet wide, which was continued within the gate as a street of the same dimensions. . . . Around the whole rectangle was a high wall. . . . More than a hundred and fifty towers studded [it], which were pierced by eight gates bearing the names of Assyrian deities. . . . Huge [stone] winged bulls with human heads guarded the entrance. . . . The palace stood on a platform situated on the line of the western city wall and extended partially outside. . . . On this elevated mass was a series of buildings, large enough to contain the population of a fair-sized town, with . . . thirty courtyards and two-hundred rooms. There were two main entrances, the one which faced the city in the style of the city gates, and more elaborate, the central archway flanked by great [stone] bulls and adorned with tiling.[58]

In inaugurating the palace in 706 B.C., Sargon chose this inscription: "For me, Sargon, who dwells in this palace, may he [the god Assur] decree as my destiny, eternal life."[59] Far from eternal, the king's life ended the following year during a campaign against still another group of rebels.

Preferring to live in the more traditional Nineveh, his successors abandoned Dur-Sharrukin, which slowly fell into ruins and disappeared from sight.

Sennacherib

Though plagued by insurrections, Sargon's reign had been a strong and successful one, for in the end he was victorious over all rebels and usurpers; and at his death the empire was bigger than ever, an immense entity encompassing all of Mesopotamia and many neighboring regions. His son, Sennacherib (ca. 704–681 B.C.), managed to keep this mighty realm in one piece. But it must be stressed that he did so with great difficulty, for he was beset by his own hefty share of bloody rebellions. No sooner had the new king ascended the throne when he learned that the Chaldean usurper Merodach-Baladan had returned

Sargon's Enemies Flee

This tract from Sargon's annals (quoted in Daniel D. Luckenbill's Ancient Records of Assyria and Babylonia) *tells how the Assyrian king was successful in his second offensive, in 710 B.C., against the Chaldean usurper, Merodach-Baladan, who opted to flee to Elam rather than fight.*

"In the twelfth year of my reign, Merodach-Baladan, son of Iakini, king of Chaldea, whose settlements are situated on the secluded shore of the sea of the east [the Persian Gulf] . . . violated his oath . . . invoked in the name of the great gods and withheld his tribute. Humbanigash, the Elamite, came to his aid. . . . He prepared for battle and descended upon the land of Sumer and Akkad [southern Babylonia]. For eleven years, against the will of the gods, he held sway over Babylon, the city of the lord of the gods, and ruled it. . . . At the command of the great lord Marduk I set my chariots in order, I prepared the camp, and gave the command to advance against the hostile and wicked people of Chaldea. . . . [Those] who had cast in their lot with Merodach-Baladan . . . I overwhelmed like a flood. I let my army eat the fruit of their orchards. . . . The cities of Samuna, Babduri, fortresses which . . . the Elamite had erected . . . I overwhelmed like the onset of a storm. . . . The might of Assur [and] Marduk, which I had made to prevail against those cities, Merodach-Baladan heard of in Babylon; fear for his own safety fell upon him in his palace and he, with his allies [and] his soldiers went out [ran away] by night and turned their faces toward . . . Elam."

and again seized Babylon. Making matters worse, the Chaldean, aided by Egyptian officials, had persuaded the princes of Sidon, Ekron, Judah, and several other Palestinian states also to rebel against their Assyrian overlords.[60]

Deciding to deal with Babylonia first, Sennacherib promptly attacked that land, and Merodach-Baladan just as promptly fled a second time. But three years later, the usurper was back again. Once more the Assyrian king drove him away and recaptured Babylon, this time installing one of his sons, Assurnadinshumi, on the Babylonian throne. Yet Assyria's southern front was still not secure; six years later, in about 694 B.C., Merodach-Baladan's friends, the Elamites, invaded Babylonia and took Babylon. This was the last straw for Sennacherib. Blind with rage, he exacted vengeance in an act of unprecedented brutality—the destruction of Babylon, sacred city of the plains:

> The city and its houses, from its foundation to its top, I destroyed, I devastated, I burned with fire. The wall and outer wall, temples and gods . . . I razed and dumped them into the Arahtu Canal. Through the midst of that city I dug canals, I flooded its site with water. . . . That in the days to come the site of that city . . . might not be remembered, I completely blotted it out.[61]

In between his Babylonian expeditions, Sennacherib found time to deal with the Palestinian rebels, most prominent among them Hezekiah, king of Judah. This campaign is familiar to many people today because parts of it are described in some detail in the Bible. The second book of Chronicles, for example, states:

> Sennacherib, king of Assyria, who was besieging Lachish [south of Jerusalem] with all his forces, sent his servants to Jerusalem to Hezekiah, king of Judah, and to all the people of Judah . . . saying . . . "On what are you relying, that you stand siege in Jerusalem. . . . Do you not know what I and my fathers have done to all the peoples of other lands?"[62]

Sennacherib's annals do not describe the siege of Lachish; however, the event is depicted in pictorial detail in the spectacular bas-reliefs found in the nineteenth century by Layard in that king's palace at Nineveh. The Assyrian sculptors who created these reliefs (which are now in the British Museum in London) worked from sketches made by Sennacherib's campaign artists, who watched the siege from a nearby hill.

Assyrian slingers hurl rocks at the fortified Jewish town of Lachish in this relief from Sennacherib's palace at Nineveh.

Sennacherib's mighty and ornate edifice, the so-called Palace Without Rival at Nineveh, sprawls along the bank of the Tigris River in this modern restoration.

Further confirmation for the siege came from the 1973–1987 excavations at Lachish directed by Israeli archaeologist David Ussishkin. As scholar Roberta Harris explains:

> Ussishkin's excavations uncovered the remains of the attacker's siege ramp—the only ancient Assyrian siege ramp yet discovered. It reached up the southwest angle of the city mound to the defensive wall, where huge amounts of weapons and debris have been found. . . . To Ussishkin's surprise, he also found evidence for a Judaean counter-ramp, erected within the city in haste, and probably under fire, to give the defenders the advantage of height and to protect the walls against the onslaught of the battering rams.[63]

Despite the heroic defense attested by these finds, Lachish fell to Sennacherib; however, Jerusalem somehow survived and the Assyrians eventually withdrew after Hezekiah agreed to pay heavy tribute (including his harem and musicians!) to his adversary.

Sennacherib is also famous for enlarging and beautifying Nineveh, making it a capital city worthy of a great empire.[64] Especially noteworthy was the so-called Palace Without Rival, which he built in the northern part of the city. "The former palace I greatly enlarged," his annals proclaim. "I finished it and splendidly adorned it; to the amazement of all peoples I filled it with costly equipment."[65]

Esarhaddon

Unfortunately for Sennacherib, he did not get a chance to live very long in his new palace. In 681 B.C., he was assassinated by his own sons, the youngest of whom,

A Message in Stone

From his Sennacherib's Palace Without Rival at Nineveh, *John M. Russell, of Columbia University's Department of Archaeology, describes how the decorations of the palace's throne-room suite were designed as a visual message, a reminder to foreign and native viewers alike of the king's supreme power.*

"Because it is the most important section of the palace, it might be expected that the decoration of the throne-room suite would have been planned with particular care. A look at its subjects and the principles upon which they are organized would seem to bear this out. . . . In approaching and passing through this suite, one encounters a sequence of three campaigns, beginning with Babylonia, then Palestine, and finally the Zagros. . . . It was only after the third [was completed] that Sennacherib began to call himself 'king of the world.' . . . [One prominent expert] has observed that the reliefs of Sennacherib, a king whose reign was relatively peaceful by Assyrian standards, seem 'paradoxically full of scenes of military narrative.' The paradox is only apparent, however, for an ever-popular method of maintaining peace is through the threat of war, and this would be the effect of these scenes of conquest, at least for that component of the audience composed of potentially disruptive foreigners. For members of the court, these images would serve as a gratifying record of Assyrian triumphs and simultaneously as a reminder that the king controls the army, the bulwark of power in Assyria."

Esarhaddon (ca. 680–669 B.C.), ascended the throne after fighting and defeating his brothers:

I entered into Nineveh, my royal city, joyfully, and took my seat upon the throne of my father. . . . The soldiers, the sinners who had fomented the plot to seize the rulership of Assyria for my brothers . . . I laid a heavy penalty upon them, I destroyed their seed [families].[66]

Esarhaddon's eleven-year reign was one of the most remarkable of all the Assyrian kings, partly because he managed, mostly through diplomacy, to keep his huge empire largely at peace. His first major act—the rebuilding of Babylon—set a remarkable precedent, signifying to all that he was more interested in *con*structive than *de*structive enterprises. The immense project continued throughout his reign, and the end results were a larger, more magnificent city and a new spirit of reconciliation with its people:

I summoned all of my artisans and the people of Babylonia in their totality.

. . . In choice oil, honey, butter, wine . . . I laid its [the city's] foundation walls. I raised the headpad to my own head and carried it [i.e., as a symbolic gesture he carried the first load of stone himself]. . . . I built [Babylon] anew, I enlarged, I raised aloft, I made magnificent. The images of the great gods I restored and had them replaced in their shrines to adorn them forever. . . . The sons of Babylon . . . their clientship I established anew.[67]

Indeed, the restoration project won Esarhaddon the friendship of most Babylonians; except for a minor incident in 680 B.C., in which the son of the usurper Merodach-Baladan attempted to seize the town of Ur, Babylonia remained loyal to Assyria for the rest of Esarhaddon's reign.

It should not be construed from these events that Esarhaddon was a mild-mannered man who had forsaken the harsh methods of his forefathers. That he could, if provoked, brutally punish as well as forgive is illustrated by his treatment of the Phoenician city of Sidon, which made the mistake of rebelling. Esarhaddon swiftly crushed the revolt, beheaded Sidon's ruler, tore down the city, and deported its surviving inhabitants to Assyria. These dire acts set the desired example, and the Mediterranean coast remained quiet for several years thereafter.

Eventually, in fact, the whole empire became relatively quiet. At this juncture, Esarhaddon saw an opportune moment to realize a goal that many Assyrian kings had dreamed of, but that none had been in a position to fulfill—the conquest of Egypt. With a civilization almost as old as Mesopotamia's, Egypt had once been a powerful nation. But in recent centuries, it

had grown weak. Though still influential enough to goad various Assyrian vassals into rebelling, the Egyptians lacked the military resources to stop Esarhaddon's enormous offensive, which in 671 B.C. subdued the capital, Memphis, and most of the countryside surrounding it in less than a month. "Without cessation I slew multitudes of his men," Esarhaddon later said about the Egyptian king, Taharqa (also Taharka or Taharqo),

> and him I smote five times with the point of my javelin. . . . Memphis, his royal city, in half a day, with mines, tunnels, assaults, I besieged, I captured . . . I burned with fire. His queen, his harem, his . . . sons and daughters, his property and his goods, his horses, his cattle, his sheep, in countless numbers, I carried off to Assyria.[68]

Despite this initial success, Esarhaddon found it difficult to maintain control over the proud Egyptians. Two years after the departure of the main Assyrian army, Taharqa, who had fled far to the south, returned, recaptured Memphis, and staged a full-scale rebellion. While on his way back to Egypt to quell this disturbance, Esarhaddon died unexpectedly, and his son, the crown prince Assurbanipal, succeeded him.

Assurbanipal

Assurbanipal (ca. 668–627 B.C.) inherited from his father the Assyrian Empire at its height, a vast realm stretching from the Nile valley in the southwest to central Armenia in the north, a distance of over one thousand miles. That realm was far from stable, of course, since Egypt was in open rebellion, and the new king realized that he had to crush the rebels as fast as possible; so he hastily made his way through Syria and Palestine, gathering troops from the subject states along the way, and entered Egypt. There, according to his annals:

> Taharqa, king of Egypt . . . heard of the advance of my army, in Memphis, and mustered his fighting men against me, offering armed resistance and battle. With the help of Assur . . . [and] the great gods . . . who advance at my side, I defeated his army in a battle on the open plain. . . . The terrible splendor of Assur and Ishtar overcame him and he went mad. . . . He forsook Memphis and fled to Thebes.[69]

The Assyrians pursued Taharqa to Thebes, located several hundred miles south (up-stream and therefore in "Upper Egypt"), which had so far remained outside the zone of Assyrian control. Taharqa fled again and about two years later died in exile. His son, Tanuatamun, then took up his cause. As soon as the main body of the Assyrian army had vacated the country, the young man gathered some patriotic native forces, marched north, and boldly liberated Memphis. But his triumph proved short-lived. Assurbanipal entered Egypt a second time, retook Memphis, and proceeded to sack and destroy Thebes. The tables were turned still again, however, when about ten years later, in 655 B.C., another Egyptian patriot, Psamtik (or Psammetichus), succeeded in driving the Assyrian occupation forces out of the country, chasing them all the way to Ashdod, in Palestine.

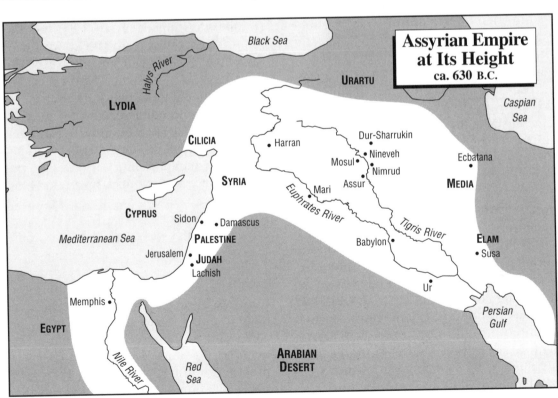

As Assyrian monarchs so often did as a matter of course, Assurbanipal would probably have attempted to put down this new rebellion. But at that moment he was involved in a major war with Elam, on his southeastern front. He managed to drive the Elamites back into their own country in fairly short order. No sooner had he done so, however, when the region flared up again. This time the trouble spot was Babylon, and the culprit was Assurbanipal's own brother, Shamashshumukin. On becoming king, Assurbanipal had agreed to his father's dying wish, namely to allow Shamashshumukin to sit on the Babylonian throne with authority second only to the imperial ruler in Nineveh. The arrangement had worked for seventeen years; but in that interval Shamashshumukin had become Babylonianized—estranged from Assyrian affairs—and now wanted to fight his brother for ultimate power over the Near East.

Assurbanipal must be given credit for attempting to defuse the crisis nonviolently. In a carefully worded appeal to the Babylonian people, he stated:

> I have heard all these empty words which that unbrotherly brother of mine has told you. . . . They are but wind; do not believe him! . . . Now by all means, do not listen to his empty words, do not spoil your reputation which is so good in my own eyes and in the eyes of all the countries, and do not sin against the god! . . . I am writing to you that you should not sully yourselves through this affair.[70]

For reasons unknown, the Babylonians rejected this offer of conciliation, and full-scale war soon broke out. Some Babylonian towns backed Shamashshumukin, while others more wisely sided with Assurbanipal, who clearly had the best chance of winning. The ancient town of Ur, for instance, sent this appeal to the Assyrian king:

> There is not a city there [in the region of Akkad] which has remained loyal to Assyria except Ur and Kisik and Shattina; and the king our lord knows that Ur has been upright [loyal] in the midst of Akkad from the first. . . . Distress is everywhere. We shall fall into their [the rebels'] hands. . . . Let the king our lord send troops for the protection of his temples . . . [otherwise] the land will slip away from the hand of the king.[71]

But the land did not slip from Assurbanipal's hand. After three years of bloodshed, the rebellion collapsed, and Shamashshumukin, in despair, set fire to his own palace and died in the blaze.

The Beginning of the End

Not long after regaining control of Babylonia, Assyria found itself in another war with Elam. This time that nation received the full brunt of Assurbanipal's unleashed wrath, as his armies swept into its heartland and in a terrifying orgy of destruction, quite literally erased it from the face of the earth. Thus did the three-thousand-year-old rivalry between Elam and the peoples of Mesopotamia end with frightening suddenness and finality.

Ironically, this pivotal event turned out to be Assyria's great turning point, the beginning of its own sudden and final end. Late in 639 B.C., the very year that Elam

Assurbanipal Ravages Elam

These are excerpts from the surviving official account of Assurbanipal's destructive campaign into Elam (quoted from Daniel D. Luckenbill's Ancient Records of Assyria and Babylonia*), which ended with that nation's annihilation.*

"The temple tower of Susa . . . I destroyed. . . . The sanctuaries of Elam I destroyed totally. Its gods and goddesses I scattered to the winds. . . . The tombs of their earlier and later kings, who did not fear Assur . . . and who had plagued the kings, my fathers, I destroyed. . . . I exposed them to the sun. Their bones I carried off to Assyria. . . . I devastated the provinces of Elam. Salt . . . I scattered over them. . . . In a month of days I ravaged Elam to its farthest border. The noise of people, the tread of cattle and sheep, the glad shouts of rejoicing, I banished from its fields. Wild asses, gazelles and all kinds of beasts of the plain, I caused to lie down among them, as if at home."

In a relief from Assurbanipal's palace, Assyrian warriors take a meal break during their siege of the Elamite city of Hamanu.

ceased to exist, Assurbanipal's royal annals fell silent, leaving the last twelve years of his reign in utter darkness, at least from the Assyrian vantage. Scattered foreign sources suggest that a combination of invasions, rebellions, and civil strife on a scale larger than the Assyrians had ever experienced began to engulf their empire. The approaching apocalypse was perhaps inevitable. The truth, after all, was that every one of Assyria's subject states and foreign neighbors hated Assyria and would gain from its elimination. Those who were familiar with a Jewish prophecy of the time must have longed to see its fulfillment:

All who look on you [Assyrians] will shrink from you and say, wasted is Nineveh; who will bemoan her? . . . The fire [will] devour you, the sword will cut you off. . . . All who hear the news of [your destruction will] clap their hands over you. For upon whom has not come your unceasing evil?[72]

5 A Society Subservient to Gods and Kings: Assyrian Life and Culture

In surveying the violent political history of the Sargonid period, in which the Assyrian Empire reached its greatest extent of power, one can easily get the impression that all aspects of Assyrian life revolved around warfare and strife. But this is an artificial impression derived in large degree from the selective nature of the surviving records. A great many of these records consist of royal annals and other official descriptions of military campaigns and construction projects, the traditional mode of expression for Assyrian monarchs. The sculptures dispersed lavishly around the halls of a king's palace, Near Eastern scholar L. Delaporte points out,

> had no other object but to glorify him personally. The texts which accompanied the sculptures likewise extolled his glory. . . . They normally consist of three main sections. The first is a panegyric [list of praises] on the king and gives a summary of his deeds . . . the next recounts the events of the reign—wars and building undertakings; the last is made up of curses upon anyone who should destroy the inscription.[73]

Besides these accounts of kingly deeds, a number of personal letters, legal contracts, and religious and scientific compositions have survived, the largest collection of which were discovered in 1849 by Layard at Nineveh. This archive, consisting of more than twenty-five thousand cuneiform tablets, constituted the bulk of the library gathered by Assurbanipal. Though valuable, most of these records deal with political, religious, and commercial affairs in royal, official, priestly, and well-to-do circles and tell very little about the everyday lives of average Assyrians. As Professor Roux remarks, "Numerous and interesting as these texts are . . . the knowledge that can be derived from them on such topics as social and economic conditions, land tenure and internal trade, for example, remains very limited and full of gaps and uncertainties."[74] When lacking direct evidence, historians usually make educated guesses, based partly on indirect clues in the existing records; partly on studying ruins, artifacts, and other archaeological finds; and also on correlations between Assyrian and Babylonian customs, since the two cultures were similar in many respects.

The King and Crown Prince

Historians know more about the king's court and imperial administration than about other aspects of Assyrian social life.

The Assyrian monarch was seen as a human being rather than as a god in human form; yet, as the god Assur's earthly representative and instrument, he was no ordinary human. Official texts frequently mention an aura or radiance surrounding his person, the *melammu*, or "awe-inspiring luminosity," presumably a supernatural force flowing directly from the god. Because of this special relationship with the divine, the king was Assur's high priest as well as the supreme head of state. For the sake of the community, it was believed, such a special person had to be closely guarded and pampered. "His person was carefully protected from disease," Oppenheim explains,

> and especially from the evil influence of magic because his well-being was considered essential for that of the country. For this reason, Assyrian kings, as we know from the letters in their archives, were surrounded by a host of diviners [those claiming to be able to foretell the future by interpreting omens] and physicians. All ominous signs were observed and interpreted with regard to their bearing on the royal person. Complex rituals existed to ward off evil signs, and at least one instance is known in Assyria where a fatal prediction was counteracted by the stratagem of making another person king . . . for one hundred days and then killing and duly burying him so that the omen should be fulfilled but fate cheated and the true king kept alive. Access to the king was carefully regulated, even for the heir apparent, to avoid untoward [adverse] encounters, and in each Assyrian palace was a room, adjacent to the throne room, for ritual ablutions [cleansings] of the king.[75]

An Assyrian high priest (left) and his king. Assyrian monarchs were supposedly surrounded by a mysterious radiance signifying their special relationship with the chief god, Assur.

The "heir apparent" was most often the king's son, the crown prince. Although the king's choice of a son as his successor was supposedly inspired by Assur and other gods, that choice had to be endorsed by other members of the royal family as well as by the nation's small elite group of noblemen. Most often these highborn people went along with the king's selection; the most famous of the few known exceptions was the power struggle among Sennacherib's sons following his murder.

Once chosen and accepted, the crown prince left his father's palace and resided in the "House of Succession," located a few miles upstream from Nineveh. There the young man learned arts and letters, received instruction in kingly duties, and prepared to replace his father at a moment's notice in case the reigning monarch should die in battle. Assurbanipal's annals contain this description of his youthful training:

> The art of the Master Adapa I learned— the hidden treasure of all scribal knowledge, the signs of heaven and earth. I was brave, I was exceedingly industrious . . . and I have studied the heavens with the learned masters of oil divination, I have solved the laborious problems of division and multiplication . . . I have read the artistic script of Sumer and the obscure Akkadian, which is hard to master. . . . I mounted my steed, I rode joyfully . . . I held the bow, I shot the arrow, the sign of my valor. I hurled heavy lances like a javelin. Holding the reins like a driver, I made the [chariot's] wheels go round. . . . At the same time I was learning royal decorum, walking in the kingly ways . . . giving commands to the nobles. . . . The father, my begetter, saw for himself the bravery which the great gods decreed as my portion.[76]

His Life No Longer His Own

Each crown prince eventually faced his day of reckoning, the moment when his father "went to his destiny." The fallen king was placed in a heavy stone sarcophagus and entombed in Assur, the oldest and most venerable Assyrian capital. After a short interval, the crown prince's coronation ceremony took place. First, servants bore him on a portable throne toward Assur's temple while a priest beat a tambourine and repeatedly shouted, "Assur is king!" Once

inside the temple, the prince offered the god sacrifices in the form of precious gifts and then prostrated himself (laid facedown) while a priest anointed him. Next, the priest solemnly bestowed on him the emblems of kingship—the crown and the scepter of Ninlil (Assur's divine spouse), all the while reciting these words:

> The diadem [crown] on your head— may Assur and Ninlil . . . put it upon you for a hundred years. . . . Before Assur, your god, may your priesthood and the priesthood of your sons find favor. With your straight scepter make your land wide. May Assur grant you quick satisfaction, justice and peace.[77]

Assurbanipal stands in his royal chariot in this wall relief found in his palace at Nineveh.

Finally, the new king proceeded to his palace, where his nobles and officials acclaimed him king and paid him homage. A national holiday and public rejoicing probably followed.

Having assumed the throne, the new king found that his life was, in a sense, no longer his own, for his duties were many and diverse. First and foremost, of course, he was the supreme commander of the army, with the authority to initiate wars at his will and to draw up plans for his military campaigns. By tradition, he also made sure army rations were distributed properly, inspected the troops, and personally led campaigns. At court, he appointed governors and other administrators, received and entertained high officials and foreign ambassadors, and dealt with a wide range of complaints by subjects. Many of these complaints were in the form of appeals for the king to dispense justice. A surviving letter captures one such appeal, from someone named Nabubalassuiqbi to King Assurbanipal:

> How does it happen that I, who have made several appeals to Your Majesty, have never been questioned by anybody? It is as if . . . I had committed a crime against Your Majesty. But I have not committed a crime against Your Majesty; I merely went . . . and conveyed an order of the king to Arrabi; although I said, "I am on business for the palace," he was so unscrupulous as to take my property away. He even arrested me and put me in fetters, and that in front of all the people. . . . Ever since last year, nobody has given me anything to eat. . . . Your Majesty should know that the same two men who took the gold jewelry from around my neck still go on planning to destroy me and to ruin me, and what terrible words about me have they made reach the ears of Your Majesty![78]

In addition to having to handle so many military and courtly duties, great and small, the king was also expected to execute his duties as high priest. These included seeing that temples were built or maintained, appointing priests, leading various religious ceremonies and festivals, and conducting numerous complicated rituals connected with omens, divination, astrology, and magic.

Differences in social status, reflected by the elaborateness of attire, are apparent in this restoration showing (left to right) a commoner, a scribe, a court official, and a nobleman.

Landowners and Workers

Although all power in Assyria theoretically resided in the king, to run an empire he naturally had to delegate some of his authority to the rich nobles who made up the

Dealing with Omens and Demons

That the Assyrian kings and nobles were obsessed with and put great store in omens, spells, curses, exorcisms, astrology, and other forms of superstition and magic is revealed in these excerpts from letters written by priests to King Esarhaddon (quoted in A. Leo Oppenheim's Letters from Mesopotamia*).*

"As to Your Majesty's request addressed to me concerning the incident with the ravens, here are the relevant omens: 'If a raven brings something into a person's house, this man will obtain something that does not belong to him. If a falcon or a raven drops something he is carrying upon a person's house or in front of a man, this house will have much traffic—traffic means profit. If a bird carries meat, another bird, or anything else, and drops it upon a person's house, this man will obtain a large inheritance.'

As to Your Majesty's writing to me concerning the ritual, they should perform the exorcistic ritual [to chase away a demon] exactly as Your Majesty did several times already. As to . . . the formulas [incantations] to be pronounced, the king should watch the formulas carefully. The king should not eat what has been cooked on fire; he should put on a loose robe of a nurse; the day after tomorrow he should go down to the river to wash himself. The king should perform the ritual . . . several times."

tiny but highly influential upper class. Besides the *tartanu,* the military officer with powers second only to the king, other important dignitaries included the palace herald, the superintendent, and the great chancellor. Apparently all but the *tartanu* acted mainly as royal advisers. Outside of the capital, there were the provincial governors *(bel pihati)* and under them an administrative chain of command including district chiefs *(rab alani)* and town "mayors" *(hazzanu)*.

All of these high officials led privileged lives, of course, residing in comfortable houses staffed by many servants and owning their own lands. In theory, all Assyrian land belonged to the king or the religious temples; in practice, however, the king and/or the temples granted high-placed persons estates as part of a reward system designed to maintain their continued homage and obedience. As a rule, such estates were not huge contiguous tracts worked by thousands of slaves, like those that developed in Roman Italy several centuries later. Most Assyrian estates were relatively small, the largest covering only about 250 acres, although a well-to-do landlord might own several such properties scattered across the empire.

Typically, such a landlord was absentee, meaning that he lived in a town or city and entrusted the upkeep of the property to a manager. Evidently the labor utilized by estate owners and managers consisted of a mixture of free agricultural workers, serfs, and perhaps a few slaves. Unfortunately the differences among these groups, as well as their precise social status and distribution remain unclear. Free workers seem sometimes to have hired themselves out to estates, although the rations they received for pay were no better than those given to unfree workers.

Some free workers probably also owned their own small plots of land; but they paid high taxes, which the government usually exacted in the form of "forced labor" rather than money. Forced labor, a common practice across the Near East, "was seen by administrators," Daniel Snell points out, "as a way of taxing peasants without having to resort to forms of money, and sometimes it was used to concentrate labor resources on a magnificent scale and to accomplish in a few years projects that otherwise might have taken generations."[79] Thus, after planting season, many Assyrian peasants must have worked off their tax burdens by devoting a few months to erecting palaces, digging canals, and other state projects.

Concerning the use of slaves and serfs in Assyria, Snell comments:

> Slaves . . . were not economically important in any ancient Near Eastern society. Police power was minimal, and these societies were not prepared to adopt the constant vigilance necessary for a slave society to flourish. Slaves came from abroad, brought in as booty in wars or as merchandise by merchants. . . . Most rich households probably had from one to five personal slaves . . . but rarely did

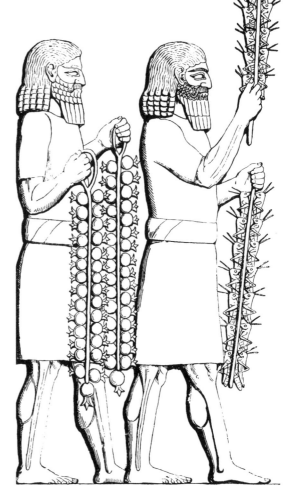

From a Nineveh wall carving, Assyrian peasants carry pomegranates and roasted locusts to a wedding banquet. Poor workers were regularly exploited by the upper classes.

> the number of slaves owned go above fifteen. Because of their propensity to run away, slaves could not efficiently be used for agricultural work, and few attempts were made in that direction. . . . [Assyrian society] also had classes of persons of low status who were not slaves but were also not free laborers. . . . The term "serf" is probably too imprecise . . . because it conjures up a European feudal system in which the peasants were not only attached to the

land . . . but also could count on the lord's political and military protection.[80]

By contrast, well-to-do Assyrian landowners were not independent warlords and had no judicial authority over the peasants who worked their estates. Whatever the differences among these various kinds of lower-class laborers, it is certain that they had at least one thing in common: like poor peasants in every age, they were all regularly exploited in one way or another by the upper classes.

Urban Life and Women

The poorer classes in Assyria, constituting the bulk of the population, typically inhabited

Assyrian Slaves

From his History of Assyria, *noted Near Eastern scholar A. T. Olmstead comments on the numbers, types, and sales of Assyrian slaves, making a distinction between domestic slaves, who were either bought or entered slavery to work off a debt, and war captives, who endured lower status and harsher treatment.*

"Domestic slaves were comparatively few in numbers. In the less wealthy families they were almost exclusively women, engaged in domestic manufacture, such as weaving, and sometimes with the status of a wife of inferior grade [in the cases of men who kept concubines as second wives]. This situation is reflected in the price of a female slave, which is regularly as high as the male. Only the few great houses possessed any large number of male slaves, and in all probability they were mostly eunuchs [castrated men]. The largest number of slaves in the possession of a private individual is thirty, and that is near the end of the empire. In great part, the slaves were married, lived in their own houses, carried on their own business, and only paid their yearly 'tribute' to their master according to fixed custom. . . . Aside from [this] annual tribute . . . their only disqualification seems to have been their inability to choose their own masters and the necessity of remaining more or less closely under that master's oversight. Thus the slave was merely a source of assured income to his master. . . . Quite different was the fate of the unfortunates who had been enslaved in war. . . . Heavily shackled and whipped on by the overseer, they labored at building palace platforms or other kinds of rude work. . . . Family groups form a considerable proportion of the slave sales, and it has even been suggested that the slave was never sold without his family."

extremely humble dwellings. In the countryside, these were most often organized into small villages. The most primitive houses were circular huts made of intertwined branches covered with thatch and loosely cemented with dried mud. The wooden or thatched door hung on a pivot secured to a post driven into the ground or attached to the wall. Stables and sheepfolds were also constructed using this method. Somewhat more permanent homes were fashioned from bricks made of clay that had been mixed with straw and either dried in the sun or baked in a kiln. Baked bricks were sturdier and lasted longer, but they were more expensive to produce and so their use was generally restricted to the larger homes of the well-to-do or to state building projects.[81]

Larger homes, including those of absentee landlords, were typically located in the cities. Compared to most other societies of the early first millennium B.C., Assyria was highly urbanized; that is, it had many towns with populations in the tens of thousands. Surrounding the imposing temples and palaces that dominated these urban centers stretched large clusters of closely packed mud-brick houses, shops, stables, and storerooms. Many of the poorer residents probably worked the plots of farmland that typically surrounded the city walls. Other urban dwellers labored inside the city walls, as artisans, traders, shopkeepers, and "factory" workers. The factories were apparently state-run workrooms in which small or large groups of people wove carpets, embroidered clothes, or produced other goods for use by the residents of the palace and/or local nobles.

Some evidence suggests that a high proportion of such factory workers were women (many of whom were also slaves). As in all ancient societies, in Assyria women were generally subservient to men. There may have been exceptions to this rule, since information about the lower classes is lacking; and it is possible that women in poor farm households shared equally in the decision making with their husbands. What little is known for certain relates to upper-class urban women (who were seen as more respectable than prostitutes and barmaids, who also resided in the cities). Assyriologist Georges Contenau summarizes the social obligations of a respectable daughter/mother:

> Until the time of her marriage a girl remained under the protection of her father, who was free to settle her in marriage exactly as he thought fit. . . .

The ivory head of an upper-class Assyrian woman, found at Nimrud and dated to about 720 B.C.

Marriage was preceded by the cere-mony of betrothal, during which the girl's future husband poured perfume on her head and brought her presents and provisions. Thereafter the girl was so fully a member of her future hus-band's family that, if he died, she would marry one of his brothers, or, if he had no brothers, one of his near relatives. The actual marriage . . . took the form of a delivery of the wife to her husband. . . . The ceremony was ac-companied by a proper marriage con-tract, which helped to give the woman the title of wife. If this formality were omitted, cohabitation over a period of two years . . . was regarded as the equiv-alent of a contract. Married life might involve either the wife's staying in her father's house or her going with her husband to his. In the former case, the husband gave the wife a sum called the *dumaki* towards the maintenance of the house, and if the husband died this contribution remained the widow's property only if the deceased had left neither sons nor brothers. . . . If, on the other hand, the young couple went to live in the husband's house, the wife brought with her a *shirqu* . . . or dowry. . . . The *shirqu* . . . remained the in-alienable property of her children, and her husband's brothers had no claim on it.[82]

Assyrian Arts

It is highly unlikely that respectable upper-class women worked in factories or as arti-sans, since the social elite generally saw menial labor as beneath them. Ironically,

Monumental stone statues of human-headed, winged bulls, like this one, weighing perhaps forty tons, often guarded the gates and throne rooms of Assyrian palaces.

the lives and works of most of the elite are long since forgotten, while the works of many nameless lower-class artisans have en-dured and come to be seen as the greatest cultural achievements of Assyrian civiliza-tion. Of Assyria's surviving arts, without doubt the most striking and original were the magnificent carved stone bas-reliefs that adorned the walls of the royal palaces. In room after room, corridor after corri-dor, many thousands of feet of reliefs bore detailed scenes of the king's life and ex-ploits. In some, he can be seen dining in picturesque gardens laden with fruit trees; in others, he hunts lions or receives tribute from vassals; and in still others, he leads his armies in battle. About the exquisite quality of these works, Chester Starr remarks:

> From the artistic point of view Assyrian relief was the highest point thus far reached in Near Eastern art. Sieges and battles at times had almost a sense of space, and in the scenes of hunting animals were shown with more realism than had ever before been achieved. Here the artists gave a vivid sense of motion, even at times of pity for the dying lions or wild asses; in other scenes the king, with fringed robe, long curled beard, and heavy shoulders and legs, was a static but powerful figure. Not until we come to Roman imperial art shall we find again artists who concentrated upon seizing the specific quality of individual historical events.[83]

Other noteworthy products of Assyrian artists included painted scenes, some on brightly colored glazed bricks used to decorate the temples and palaces, others on plaster, forming lively wall murals in both public buildings and private residences. Surviving examples display tremendous skill and freedom of expression and are by no means artistically inferior to the carved reliefs. Assyrian artisans also turned out beautiful metal artifacts, including bronze, silver, and gold plates, drinking vessels, and ornaments. And their work in sculpted ivory was equally fine; excavators have brought to light ivory-decorated thrones, beds, chairs, and doors, as well as ivory bowls, jewelry boxes, vases, pins, spoons, and combs, many of them inlaid with precious stones. With the notable exception of the gigantic human-headed and winged bulls and lions that guarded the palace gates and throne rooms, few freestanding statues have been found.

Astronomy and Medicine

Unlike stone, metal, and ivory artifacts, which sometimes survive for thousands of years, papyrus parchment—on which Mesopotamian peoples kept most of their everyday letters, memoranda, mathematical and astronomical calculations, and medical observations—deteriorates quickly. Therefore, much information about Assyrian astronomy and medicine has been lost. Luckily, the surviving portions of Assurbanipal's library contain a number of cuneiform tablets relating to these disciplines. These suggest that Assyrian astronomers and doctors made no new or original contributions, but merely carried on traditions borrowed from Babylonia, long the main cultural model for Assyria and other Mesopotamian nations.

The Babylonian division of the year into twelve lunar months, for instance, was standard throughout Mesopotamia. Professor Roux explains:

> The year began on the first New Moon following the spring equinox and was divided into twelve months of twenty-nine or thirty days. Each day began at sunset and was divided into twelve "double-hours," themselves divided into sixty "double-minutes"—a system which we still follow and owe to the Babylonians. Unfortunately, the lunar year is shorter than the solar year by approximately eleven days, so that after nine years the difference amounts to one full season. . . . For centuries the difficulty created by the difference between the solar year and the lunar year was solved arbitrarily, the king deciding that one or two intercalary [extra inserted] months should be added to the year [on a periodic basis].[84]

Like their Babylonian counterparts, Assyrian astronomers, most or all of them priests, kept close watch on the heavens, noting the regular movements of the sun, moon, and planets through the twelve signs (constellations) of the zodiac. Their instruments were crude by modern standards. These included the gnomon (a rudimentary sundial), the clepsydra (a clock operated by moving water), and the polos (a device that measured the shadow of a tiny ball suspended over a half-sphere). Through patient, repetitive, and accurate celestial observations, these observers gathered data that they then interpreted in terms of omens and planetary influences on future human events.[85] Assyrian kings, themselves priests, put great store in such predictions, often planning important events and undertakings around them.

In the medical field, the Assyrians, like the Babylonians, believed that sickness and disease were inflicted by the gods to punish human sins. In this view, the gods might strike a person directly, bringing on sudden illness; and doctors recognized certain symptoms as characteristic of one god or another. Or the gods might allow demons to take control of a person's body, or sorcerers and witches to cast spells on him or her. Not surprisingly, magical rites, incantations, prayers, and sacrifices were the principal remedies in this traditional magical-religious brand of medicine, referred to as *ashiputu*.

At least by the Sargonid period, a few doctors also practiced a more practical kind of medicine, called *asutu*. Although they, too, believed in divine wrath and evil demons, and certainly knew nothing about the existence of germs, they did recognize that some sickness is caused by natural agents, such as dust, spoiled food or drink, or infectious "contagion." And they accordingly attempted to treat some patients with various drugs, herbs, ointments, and perhaps some simple kinds of surgery.

The fresh approach used by these practical healers represents the first stirrings of true scientific inquiry based on evidence and cause and effect, which would begin to find fuller expression a few centuries later in Greece. For the moment, Assyrian medicine, like other aspects of daily life in Mesopotamia, was largely locked into and dictated by age-old traditions that emphasized the subservience of society and its members to the immortal gods and their earthly representative, the king.

A lion-headed, eagle-footed Assyrian-Babylonian disease demon holds the mace of wounding and dagger of killing.

Chapter

6 A Colossus with Feet of Clay: Assyria's Sudden Collapse

Early in 639 B.C., when Assyria defeated and annihilated its old foe Elam, King Assurbanipal must have felt jubilant, invulnerable, and secure. He and his immediate predecessors, the first three Sargonids, had managed to gain victory over nearly every adversary and to crush rebellion after rebellion across their huge empire. Only Egypt had managed to shake off the Assyrian yoke; and it is certain that Assurbanipal, having secured his eastern frontier, planned to remedy that situation in short order. On the surface, it seemed that the Assyrian realm might be nearly invincible and that it would continue to dominate and terrorize the Near East for generations to come.

Yet as it turned out, Assyrian invincibility was merely an illusion. Over the years, Assyria had undertaken innumerable campaigns and invasions; expended vast amounts of human and material resources, many of which it had looted from the conquered; and all the while attempted the gargantuan task of holding together, literally at swordpoint, hundreds of far-flung and endlessly rebellious peoples and cities. The end result was that the Assyrian state had fatally overextended itself. Instead of making friends and alliances among neighbors, the Assyrians had deliberately pursued a policy of war, destruction, and terror, turning these neighbors into bitter enemies.

Even worse, the Assyrian rulers had paid too little attention to ominous developments in the lands beyond the barrier of the Zagros range. There, the Medes, whom the masters of Assur saw as nothing more than a backward people on the fringes of civilization, were gathering strength and building a formidable military machine. That deadly vehicle would eventually roll across northern Mesopotamia and crush the Assyrian heartland. Thus, as the mighty Assyrian Empire basked confident in the

In this dramatic representation from one of the many wall reliefs found in his palace, Assurbanipal, Assyria's last great king, slays a lion.

glory of Assurbanipal's victories, "it suddenly became apparent," quips Georges Roux, "that the colossus had feet of clay."[86]

Internal Strife, External Threats

Because Assurbanipal's annals ceased after the fateful year 639 B.C., it is impossible to reconstruct the exact nature of the troubles he and his country experienced during the remainder of his reign. However, the surviving texts of his immediate successors, though fragmentary, describe a land torn by civil war and internal devastation. After Assurbanipal's death in 627 B.C., two of his sons, Assur-etil-ilani ("Assur, hero of the gods") and Sin-shar-ishkun ("The god Sin has appointed the king"), fought each other for the throne. Apparently, Assur-etil-ilani, about which almost nothing is known, won this bout and ruled for about four years, taking up residence in the palace in Nimrud. Whether he died in battle, of natural causes, or was murdered is unknown; what is certain is that his brother, Sin-shar-ishkun, assumed power in 623 B.C. A mangled section of one of the new king's annals alludes to cities damaged in the civil conflict and to his "opponent," almost certainly his dead brother:

> At the beginning of my kingship, in my first year of reign, when I seated myself upon the royal throne, to rehabilitate the [wrecked] metropolises [cities], to restore completely the sanctuaries, walls, and habitations of Assyria* . . . steadfastly I* . . . and the great gods, whose divinity I worship, have exposed

my cause against my opponent, and upon the plain* . . . they have.*[87]

With Assyria reeling from internal strife and disorder, it simultaneously found itself facing steadily mounting external threats. All over the Near East, its subjects and vassals took advantage of its troubles, either severing ties with the central authority in Nineveh or simply ignoring it. As the crisis worsened, the most potent and immediate danger to Assyria came from its longtime alter ego, Babylonia, where, in 626 B.C., a Chaldean named Nabopolassar ousted the Assyrian garrison from the capital and seized the throne. This marked the inauguration of Babylon's greatest and most famous dynasty, the Chaldean (or Neo-Babylonian), which would rule lower Mesopotamia in splendor for nearly a century.

Nabopolassar had not forgotten the humiliations his ancestors, including Merodach-Baladan, had suffered in their failed attempts to liberate Babylonia from Assyrian domination. Once firmly in control in Babylon, Nabopolassar carried on the war, driving the Assyrians out of one Babylonian city after another. By about 616 B.C., he felt ready to move against Assyria itself, and his advance along the Euphrates was captured in the Babylonian chronicle of his reign:

> In the tenth year [of his reign], Nabopolassar, in the month of *Aiaru* [April/May], mobilized the Babylonian army and marched up the bank of the Euphrates. . . . In the month of *Abu* [July/August] they reported that the Assyrian army was in the city of Kablini. Nabopolassar went up against them. . . . He made an attack upon the Assyrian army. The army of Assyria

---

Editor's Note: The * indicates missing or unreadable text in ancient works.

Siege and Countersiege

"In the eleventh year [of Nabopolassar's reign], the king of Akkad [Babylonia] mobilized his army and marched up the bank of the Tigris. In the month [of] *Aiaru* [April/May] he encamped by the city of Assur. On the [?] day of *Simanu* [May/June] he made an attack upon the city but did not take the city. The king of Assyria mobilized his army and, the king of Akkad being turned back from Assur, pursued him, along the Tigris, as far as the city of Tekrit. The king of Akkad took his army up into the fortress of Tekrit. The king of Assyria and his army encamped against the army of the king of Akkad which was shut up in Tekrit. For ten days he made attacks upon them but did not take the city. The army of the king of Akkad . . . inflicted a decisive defeat upon Assyria. The king of Assyria and his army gave up and returned to his land."

. . . sustained a decisive defeat. They took many of them prisoners . . . and [many of] the nobles of Assyria they captured.[88]

Nabopolassar also laid siege to the city of Assur, but he failed to take it. An indication of just how desperate Assyria was at this moment was the appeal for aid made by King Sin-shar-ishkun to none other than Egypt, one of the chief former victims of Assyrian aggression. Possibly because they feared the rising power of Babylonia more than the now-faltering might of Assyria, the Egyptians temporarily put aside their anti-Assyrian grudge and agreed to send help. With Egyptian backing, perhaps Assyria might have effected some sort of peaceful compromise with Babylonia and

thereby saved itself from destruction. However, two factors worked against this scenario. First, Egypt did not dispatch troops in time to make a difference; second, and more important, it was at this crucial juncture that the rapidly changing Mesopotamian power game was suddenly dealt a political-military wild card—the advance of the Medes.

The Rise of Media

Even as the Assyrian kings began to spread their harsh rule over large sections of the Near East in the ninth century B.C., the seeds of their destruction had already been planted in the uplands of the Iranian plateau. Perhaps sometime between 1100 and 1000 B.C., during the second Mesopotamian dark age, small groups identifying themselves as "Aryans" descended from the steppe lands west and north of the Caspian Sea and onto the upland plateau east of the Zagros range. The name Iran, which later came to identify the region, is derived from the word *aryanam*, meaning "land of the Aryans." Among these peoples were the Medes, at first a loose confederation of tribes that grew more populous and powerful during the same years that the Assyrian Empire was expanding across the Near East.

By the mid–eighth century, the two peoples were already engaged in periodic wars, as recorded in the annals of the Assyrian monarchs Tiglathpileser III and Sargon II. After defeating various Median groups, Assyria signed treaties supposedly bringing them into the Assyrian realm. One such treaty, agreed to by Esarhaddon and a Median leader named Ramataia in about 672 B.C., has survived and reads in part:

> This is the treaty that Esarhaddon, king of the world, king of Assyria . . . concludes with Ramataia, prince of the city of Urakazabarna. . . . This is the treaty that Esarhaddon . . . has concluded with you in the presence of the great gods of heaven and earth concerning Assurbanipal, the crown prince, son of your lord Esarhaddon, who he has named and appointed as crown prince. When Esarhaddon . . . dies . . . he [Assurbanipal] will exercise the kingship and sovereignty of Assyria over you. You shall protect him in town and country: you shall fight and die for him. . . . You shall not be hostile to him, nor . . . rise against him or under-

take anything against him that is not good and seemly.[89]

Despite such agreements, the peoples of the Iranian plateau, far from the central authority in Nineveh and difficult to police, remained largely independent of Assyrian control; and the Median chieftains continued a process already well under way, namely the unification of their respective tribes into a formidable nation. Local kings named Deioces (ca. 700–647 B.C.?) and his son Phraortes (ca. 647–625 B.C.?) appear to have been the two key architects of this endeavor. The Greek historian Herodotus described how Deioces created a kingship and an impressive new capital city:

> Deioces' first act was to command his subjects to build a palace worthy of a

A Median noble couple. The Medes, who eventually overthrew the Assyrian Empire, originally inhabited the highlands of the Iranian plateau, there building their strongly fortified capital of Ecbatana.

king, and to grant him the protection of a private guard. The Medes complied; they built a large and well-defended palace on a site he himself indicated, and allowed him to select a bodyguard without restriction of choice. Once firmly on the throne, Deioces put pressure on the Medes to build a single great city to which, as the capital of the country, all other towns were to be held of secondary importance. Again they complied, and the city now known as Ecbatana was built, a place of great size and strength fortified by concentric walls, these so planned that each successive circle was higher than the one below it by the height of the battlements. . . . The circles are seven in number, and the innermost contains the royal palace and treasury. . . . The battlements of the five outer rings are painted in different colors, the first white, the second black, the third crimson, the fourth blue, the fifth orange; the battlements of the two inner rings are plated with silver and gold respectively. These fortifications were to protect the king and his palace; the people had to build their houses outside the circuit of the walls.[90]

This rise in Median unity and power culminated in the accession in 625 B.C. of Cyaxares II, the dynamic ruler who was destined finally to defeat the Assyrians and in the process to launch the Median Empire. According to Herodotus, the key to Cyaxares' success was his program of military expansion and reorganization, which he instituted immediately after succeeding his father, Phraortes. Cyaxares divided his spearmen, archers, and cavalry into distinct units, each of which was trained separately and used in a specific manner on the battlefield. He also instituted standardized military uniforms, consisting of a long-sleeved leather tunic that ended above the knee, held by a double belt with a round buckle; leather trousers; laced shoes with projecting tips; and on the head, a round felt cap with a neck flap. Archers, and also some soldiers who used both spear and bow, carried their bows in very elaborate cases and kept their arrows in leather quivers that hung from the shoulder or waist. Although many of Cyaxares' troops were native Medes, he also drew upon recruits from minor Iranian peoples whom Media had recently conquered and now held as vassals.

A Wave of Destruction

When Cyaxares was confident that his army was large and formidable enough, he laid his plans for an assault on Assyria, which, he knew, had grown weak in recent years. In 615 B.C., less than a year after Babylonia's Nabopolassar began his own offensive against the Assyrians, Cyaxares' forces suddenly swept out of the Zagros foothills and took the town of Arrapha, about sixty miles east of Assur. Meeting surprisingly little resistance, the Medes followed up the following year with an attack on Assur itself, the oldest and most sacred of Assyria's cities. The Babylonian chronicle records this event: "[The Median king] descended the Tigris, encamped against Assur, made an assault upon the city and captured it. The city he destroyed. He inflicted a bad defeat on the people and nobles."[91]

Hearing of the Medes' march on Assur, Nabopolassar rushed his troops to the scene, hoping to take part in the attack and share in the victory spoils; but he arrived too late. Nevertheless, he and Cyaxares both saw the wisdom of an alliance against their mutual foe. There, in Assur's ruins, they signed a pact and soon afterward sealed it by bringing together in marriage Nabopolassar's son, Nebuchadrezzar, and the Median princess Amytis.

Perhaps by applying all of its remaining resources in an all-out effort, Assyria might have been able to hold its own against either the Babylonians or the Medes acting alone. Confronted with the alliance between these formidable opponents, however, the Assyrian Empire was doomed. In the summer of 612 B.C., Nabopolassar's and Cyaxares' forces poured into the Assyrian heartland north of Assur, taking town after town. Reaching Nimrud, they stormed the protective fort that Shalamaneser III had built in the ninth century B.C., a structure that had come to be used as a storehouse for treasures and cuneiform tablets. Archaeologists have found many spearheads and other weapons around the base of the walls, evidence of the desperate, bloody fighting that raged as the attackers swarmed over the battlements. Inside the central storeroom, the six-foot-thick ash layer the excavators encountered attests to the severity of the fire the victors lit as they viciously laid waste to the once great city.

This wave of destruction finally reached the gates of Assyria's largest and most important city—Nineveh. A badly fragmented section of the Babylonian chronicle briefly describes the city's fall:

A modern portrait of King Nebuchadrezzar, whose father, Nabopolassar, helped the Medes rid the Near East of the widely hated Assyrians. No one knows what either man actually looked like.

The king of Akkad [Babylonia]* . . . and Cyaxares* . . . they went along the bank of the Tigris and* . . . in Nineveh* . . . a mighty assault [they] made upon the city. In the month of *Abu*, the city was taken* . . . a great slaughter was made of the people and nobles. On that day Sin-shar-ishkun, king of Assyria, fled from the city. . . . Great quantities of spoil from the city . . . they carried off. The city they turned into a mound and ruin heap.[92]

After the news of Nineveh's destruction reached faraway Judah, the prophet Nahum penned this more vivid and famous description of the chaos and bloodshed accompanying that momentous event:

Editor's Note: The * indicates missing or unreadable text in ancient works.

The shatterer [Cyaxares? Nabopolassar? The hand of God?] has come up against you. Man the ramparts . . . collect all your strength. . . . The shield of his mighty men is red, his soldiers are clothed in scarlet. The chariots flash like flame when mustered in array; the chargers prance. The chariots rage in the streets, they rush to and fro through the squares; they gleam like torches, they dart like lightning. . . . The river gates are opened, the palace is in dismay; its mistress [the queen?] is stripped, she is carried off, her maidens lamenting. . . . Nineveh is like a pool whose waters run away. "Halt! Halt!" they cry; but none turns back. Plunder the silver, plunder the gold! There is no end of treasure, or wealth of every precious thing. Desolate! Desolation and ruin! Hearts faint and knees tremble, anguish is on all loins, all faces grow pale![93]

The Last Stand

Though the invaders had converted the main Assyrian cities to smoldering heaps of rubble, their task was not yet finished. Sin-shar-ishkun perished somehow, perhaps at the hands of his own officers; and one of these officers now claimed the throne, taking the name of King Assuruballit, who some seven hundred years before had launched Assyria's first empire by seizing parts of the fallen Mitannian kingdom. The new Assuruballit hastily scraped together the Assyrian troops who had survived the capture of the heartland, fled westward, and made a last stand at Harran, on the upper reaches of the Euphrates.

There he was reinforced by a regiment of Egyptian troops, who had finally arrived in fulfillment of the Assyrian-Egyptian alliance concluded about four years prior. In 610 B.C., according to the Babylonian chronicle, the Medes and Babylonians advanced on Harran:

In the sixteenth year [of Nabopolassar's reign] . . . the king of Akkad mobilized his army and . . . [the Medes] came to the support of Akkad and they united their armies and toward Harran, against Assuruballit, who sat on the throne in Assyria, they marched. Assuruballit and the army of Kullania [likely the Egyptian commander], which had come to his aid—fear of the enemy fell upon them and they forsook the city.[94]

The chronicle suggests that not long after fleeing, Assuruballit returned and attempted to retake Harran, but that he was unsuccessful. And thereafter, he, the throne, and what little was left of the Assyrian government were simply heard of no more.

The brief but fearsome Babylonian-Median campaign was so shattering that Assyria's heartland, which had remained continuously inhabited and prosperous for almost two thousand years, lay devastated; the last remnants of the once huge and mighty empire ruled from that heartland quickly fell to pieces; and in the decades and centuries that followed, all that remained of that realm was the memory of its cruelty. Nabopolassar himself made reference to the fear and damage Assyria had so long wrought throughout the Near East in a statement that could be taken as an epitaph for the fallen masters of Assur:

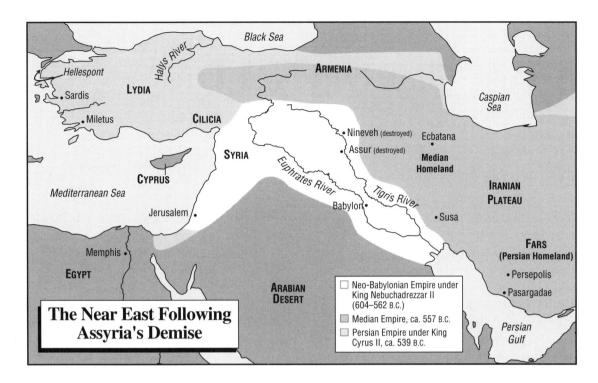

The Near East Following Assyria's Demise

Neo-Babylonian Empire under King Nebuchadrezzar II (604–562 B.C.)

Median Empire, ca. 557 B.C.

Persian Empire under King Cyrus II, ca. 539 B.C.

I slaughtered the land of Assyria, I turned the hostile land into heaps and ruins. The Assyrian, who since distant days had ruled over all the peoples and with his heavy yoke had brought injury to the people of the Land [Babylonia], their feet from Akkad I turned back; their yoke I threw off.[95]

Zephaniah, great-grandson of Hezekiah, the Jewish ruler whom Sennacherib had forced to pay humiliating tribute, left behind another epitaph for a people whose most tangible legacy was the undying hatred of their neighbors:

And he [the Lord] will stretch out his hand against the north, and destroy Assyria; and he will make Nineveh a desolation, a dry waste like the desert. Herds shall lie down in the midst of her, all the beasts of the field; the vulture and the hedgehog shall lodge in her capitals; the owl shall hoot in the window, the raven croak on the threshold; this is the exultant city that dwelt secure, that said to herself, "I am and there is none else." What a desolation she has become, a lair for wild beasts! Everyone who passes by her hisses and shakes his fist.[96]

As for the Assyrian people, those who managed to survive the fall of their country must have eked out whatever livings they could in the shadows of their new masters and wondered why the great god Assur had abandoned them. As the years passed, their children and their children's children were steadily and completely absorbed into the Near East's ever-churning melting pot of peoples; and very soon there were no more Assyrians left to wonder.

A Past That Did Not Die

The annihilation of the Assyrian Empire near the close of the seventh century B.C. created a new balance of power in the Near East, in which four nations of roughly the same strength dominated various regions. Media controlled southern and western Iran and parts of northern Mesopotamia; Chaldean Babylonia held sway over the rest of Mesopotamia and claimed sovereignty over some of the former Assyrian vassals in Palestine and Syria; Egypt also had designs on Palestine and Syria; and Lydia, a relatively new but rich and powerful kingdom, dominated western and central Anatolia. These nations were not content with the status quo, and inevitably disputes and wars erupted among them. Thus, the Assyrian kings were not yet cold in their graves, so to speak, when the Near East entered a new cycle of ambition, bloody conquest, and rising and falling empires.

The Newly Expansionist Babylonia

The first major face-off in the post-Assyrian political landscape was between Babylonia and Egypt over control of the Mediterranean coast. The Egyptians, who had recently moved troops north in a vain at-

tempt to help the last Assyrian ruler, now controlled Syria as far north as Carchemish. Nabopolassar delegated the task of dislodging the Egyptians from that key city to his son Nebuchadrezzar, who did so in 605 B.C. Nebuchadrezzar then marched south through Palestine, demanding vassal allegiance from Judah and other states, and had nearly reached Pelusium, on Egypt's border, when the news arrived that Nabopolassar had died. The son hastened to Babylon, where he eagerly took charge of his father's crown and growing empire.

But to the new king's dismay, the newly expansionist Babylonia now began to experience some of the same troubles Assyria had in trying to hold together an empire of far-flung and diverse peoples. In the next few years, several Palestinian states, including Judah, rebelled, and Nebuchadrezzar, though he had grown up hating the Assyrians for their cruelty, now used some of the same tactics they had, including terror and deportation. Roberta Harris tells of Judah's fate after the Babylonians captured Jerusalem in 587 B.C.:

> The Babylonians first looted Jerusalem, destroying the Temple, and then set the city on fire. . . . Zedekiah [the Judaean ruler] fled the city but was captured and brought before Nebuchadrezzar at Riblah in Syria. He was

forced to witness the execution of his sons, was then blinded and taken to Babylon in chains. Many of the important citizens of Jerusalem were sent after their king into exile. . . . Whole families must have packed up their belongings on ox-carts, to make the terrible journey of several hundred miles to a strange new land.[97]

Media Eclipsed

Meanwhile, many miles to the north and east, the Medes were involved in their own program of conquest and expansion. Not long after consolidating the former northern Assyrian lands, Cyaxares' armies were

In this modern depiction of a biblical scene, Babylonia's King Nebuchadrezzar addresses his courtiers from a vantage overlooking the mighty city of Babylon.

once more on the march and by 590 B.C. had captured much of Armenia, a region in which Assyria had invested, and often wasted, many precious human and material resources. Convinced that these aggressions had made him stronger, Cyaxares, like Nebuchadrezzar, apparently did not foresee the serious problems he faced in maintaining a vast empire of discontented vassals. So in 589 B.C. the overconfident Median ruler moved farther westward and brazenly invaded the newest of the Near Eastern great powers, Lydia. The Lydian king, Alyattes, met the challenge with his own formidable army, and, according to Herodotus, the war "continued for five years during which both Lydians and Medes won a number of victories."[98]

Ironically, it was natural rather than human forces that brought the Median-Lydian war to a sudden and unexpected halt. In one of history's greatest accidents of timing, on May 28, 585 B.C., at the height of a great battle between the opposing forces, a total eclipse of the sun occurred. Herodotus later recorded: "After five years of indecisive warfare, a battle took place in which the armies had already engaged, when day was suddenly turned into night. . . . Both Lydians and Medes broke off the engagement when they saw this darkening of the day."[99] Believing the eclipse to be an omen of ill fortune, the Medes marched out of Lydia, never to return.

Cyaxares died the following year, unaware that the eclipse would indeed prove a portent of bad luck for the Medes; for their empire was itself soon eclipsed by one of their own subject peoples—the Persians. Beginning in the 550s B.C., a brilliant, charismatic, and talented Persian nobleman, Cyrus II, led a successful rebellion that quickly toppled the short-lived Median

Empire and then went on to conquer Lydia, Babylonia, and parts of Palestine. At its greatest extent, under some of Cyrus's successors, the Persian realm became the greatest empire the world had yet seen. This vast dominion, stretching from northern Greece in the west to the borders of India in the east, and from Egypt in the south to central Armenia in the north, contained literally hundreds of different peoples, ethnic groups, and languages.

Ancient Enmities Linger

Like Assyria, Persia enjoyed a period of wealth and power and then fell apart from a combination of internal problems and external threats. The Greek conqueror Alexander the Great incorporated Persia into his own empire in the late fourth century B.C. But this vast realm barely outlived its creator. Not long after Alexander's passing, his leading generals fell into a power struggle over who should succeed him. These ambitious men waged a series of devastating wars that lasted over forty years. Finally, by about 280 B.C., three large kingdoms emerged in what had been Alexander's empire; the biggest, founded by Seleucus, encompassed the former Assyrian, Babylonian, Median, and Persian homelands, along with sections of Palestine and Asia Minor.

In time, the Seleucid realm also crumbled, giving way to the Parthian Empire (ca. 140 B.C.), which in turn was absorbed by the Sassanian Empire (in A.D. 224), which itself fell to Islamic Arab armies (ca. 650). And so it continued: one conquest following another, with a constant infusion

Cyrus I, often called "the Great," who ruled Persia from 550 to 530 B.C., gave himself the title of "King of the Medes and Persians." He and his successors ruled over a vast empire that influenced the fortunes of most Near Eastern peoples for almost two centuries.

The troops of Alexander the Great, the Greek conqueror, swarm around the famous Great Sphinx after their triumphant entry into Egypt. The Egyptians, long dominated by Persia, welcomed the Greeks as liberators.

of new peoples, cultures, and beliefs, each merging with the older, traditional ones to form the highly diversified hybrid cultures of the modern Near East.

Ironically, though the gods, local customs, military weapons, and national boundaries in the region are very different today than they were in the heydays of As-

sur, Nineveh, and Babylon, ancient enmities linger. The animosities that fueled relentless wars between the peoples of the Tigris-Euphrates plains (Sumerians, Babylonians, Assyrians) and the Iranian highlands (Elamites, Medes, Persians) have their modern counterparts in recent disputes and conflicts between the nations of Iraq and Iran. And the ancient desire to march south to and control the Persian Gulf, a prime goal of conquerors from Akkad's Sargon to Assyria's Assurbanipal, was mirrored in Iraq's 1990 invasion of Kuwait, a tiny country occupying what was once southern Sumer, cradle of Mesopotamian civilization. Thus, as Daniel Snell points out, in certain ways the rich mixture of ancient Near Eastern cultures, of which Assyria was a part,

> did not die, but the texts that documented them ceased, their rulers changed, and they became slowly the societies and economies of the region today. It would be wrong to overemphasize the continuities with the past of those societies . . . but it would be equally wrong to ignore that the [present] geographical realities are similar to conditions in ancient times. . . . To [study] the distant past of these places does not give us keys to policy questions for people of the region today. . . . But it [illuminates] a very long and important part of the human past and helps us to see some of the variety and triumphs of our now dead fellows.[100]

Notes

Introduction: A People Who Lived and Died by the Sword

1. Quoted in C. W. Ceram, *Gods, Graves, and Scholars: The Story of Archaeology.* Translated by E. B. Garside and Sophie Wilkins. New York: Random House, 1986, p. 286.

2. Nahum, in Bible, 3:1, Revised Standard Version. New York: Thomas Nelson and Sons, 1952.

3. Isaiah, in Bible, 37:11, 18–19.

4. Herodotus, *The Histories.* Translated by Aubrey de Selincourt. New York: Penguin, 1972, p. 81.

5. Chester G. Starr, *Early Man: Prehistory and the Civilizations of the Ancient Near East.* New York: Oxford University Press, 1973, p. 152.

6. *Annals of Assurnasirpal,* quoted in Daniel D. Luckenbill, ed., *Ancient Records of Assyria and Babylonia.* 2 vols. Chicago: University of Chicago Press, 1926. Reprint: New York: Greenwood Press, 1968, vol. 1, p. 147.

7. Ezekiel, in Bible, 32:22–23.

8. Quoted in Ceram, *Gods, Graves, and Scholars,* pp. 291–92.

Chapter 1: Between the Great Rivers: The Early Peoples of Mesopotamia

9. A. Leo Oppenheim, *Letters from Mesopotamia: Official, Business, and Private Letters on Clay Tablets from Two Millennia.* Chicago: University of Chicago Press, 1967, pp. 2–3.

10. Daniel C. Snell, *Life in the Ancient Near East, 3100–332 B.C.* New Haven, CT: Yale University Press, 1997, p. 12.

11. Trevor Watkins, "The Beginnings of Warfare," in Sir John Hackett, ed., *Warfare in the Ancient World.* New York: Facts On File, 1989, p. 16.

12. Snell, *Life in the Ancient Near East,* p. 14.

13. The Tigris River proved harder to tame because it is faster moving, carries a larger volume of water, and is more susceptible to unpredictable, destructive flooding than the Euphrates; these factors made the Tigris more difficult to navigate in ships and to divert for irrigation. For more detailed comparisons of the two rivers, see A. Leo Oppenheim, *Ancient Mesopotamia: Portrait of a Dead Civilization.* Chicago: University of Chicago Press, 1977, pp. 40–42; and Jorgen Laessoe, *People of Ancient Assyria: Their Inscriptions and Correspondence.* Translated by F. S. Leigh-Browne. London: Routledge and Kegan Paul, 1963, pp. 12–13.

14. The name Sumer comes from the later Babylonian name for southern Babylonia, the old Sumerian heartland. The Sumerians themselves called this region Kengir, meaning "civilized land."

15. Michael Wood, *Legacy: The Search for Ancient Cultures.* New York: Sterling Publishing, 1992, p. 27.

16. In the legend, Gilgamesh was the king of Uruk. No specific evidence of his rule has been found, but, as Daniel Snell points out, "the problem of finding the historical Gilgamesh is complicated by the fact that the name Gilgamesh is almost certainly a later epithet for the hero, not the name he bore in life; it may mean 'heroic ancestor'" (Snell, *Life in the Ancient Near East,* p. 18).

17. *Epic of Gilgamesh,* quoted in Morris Jastrow, *The Civilizations of Babylonia and Assyria.* Philadelphia: J. B. Lippincott, 1915, pp. 448–50.

18. Georges Roux, *Ancient Iraq.* New York: Penguin, 1980, pp. 90–91.

19. Roux, *Ancient Iraq,* p. 92.

20. H. W. F. Saggs, *Civilization Before Greece and Rome*. New Haven, CT: Yale University Press, 1989, p. 45.

21. Watkins, "Beginnings of Warfare," in Hackett, *Warfare in the Ancient World*, p. 19.

22. Roux, *Ancient Iraq*, p. 140.

Chapter 2: A Duty to Conquer and Rule: The Rise of the Assyrian Nation

23. James Henry Breasted, *Ancient Times: A History of the Early World*. Boston: Ginn and Company, 1944, p. 180.

24. In the ancient texts, the city, kingdom, and god are all called *Ash-shur;* the terms Assur and Assyria, used routinely in this and other modern histories, are later, Latinized versions.

25. Oppenheim, *Ancient Mesopotamia*, pp. 167–68.

26. About twenty thousand cuneiform tablets were discovered at the site of ancient Mari, on the upper Euphrates, in 1935 by French excavators. Among these are about three hundred letters written by Shamshi-Adad and his sons, who briefly ruled Mari in the early eighteenth century B.C.

27. Quoted in Laessoe, *People of Ancient Assyria,* p. 43.

28. Quoted in Luckenbill, *Ancient Records of Assyria and Babylonia,* vol. 1, p. 17.

29. Quoted in Laessoe, *People of Ancient Assyria,* p. 69.

30. Quoted in Laessoe, *People of Ancient Assyria,* p. 76.

31. Watkins, "Beginnings of Warfare," in Hackett, *Warfare in the Ancient World,* p. 28.

32. Oppenheim, *Ancient Mesopotamia*, p. 65.

33. Quoted in Luckenbill, *Ancient Records of Assyria and Babylonia,* vol. 1, p. 40.

34. Quoted in Luckenbill, *Ancient Records of Assyria and Babylonia,* vol. 1, p. 51.

35. Among these proposed innovations were the new tactic of javelin throwers "swarming" chariots and their crews, thereby neutralizing them; the adoption of better protective armor by foot soldiers; and the introduction of new, deadly slashing swords. See Robert Drews, *The End of the Bronze Age: Changes in Warfare and the Catastrophe ca. 1200 B.C.* Princeton, NJ: Princeton University Press, 1993.

36. Drews, *The End of the Bronze Age,* p. 18.

37. Roux, *Ancient Iraq*, p. 247.

38. Modern historians use the Hebrew versions of the names of many Assyrian monarchs (since the Hebrew Old Testament was long the main source of these names); in this case, Tiglathpileser is the Hebrew form of the original Assyrian name Tukulti-apil-Esharra, meaning "My trust is in the son of the god Esharra (Assur)."

39. Quoted in Luckenbill, *Ancient Records of Assyria and Babylonia,* vol. 1, pp. 73–74.

Chapter 3: A Name Once More to Be Dreaded: Assyria Is Reborn

40. Roux, *Ancient Iraq*, p. 264.

41. Nahum, in Bible, 3:2–3.

42. Quoted in Luckenbill, *Ancient Records of Assyria and Babylonia,* vol. 1, p. 110.

43. Quoted in Luckenbill, *Ancient Records of Assyria and Babylonia,* vol. 1, p. 111.

44. Roux, *Ancient Iraq*, p. 267.

45. Snell, *Life in the Ancient Near East,* p. 79.

46. Quoted in Luckenbill, *Ancient Records of Assyria and Babylonia,* vol. 1, pp. 166–67.

47. Quoted in Luckenbill, *Ancient Records of Assyria and Babylonia,* vol. 1, p. 146.

48. Quoted in Oppenheim, *Letters from Mesopotamia*, pp. 176–77.

49. Drews, *The End of the Bronze Age,* p. 165.

50. Quoted in Luckenbill, *Ancient Records of Assyria and Babylonia,* vol. 1, p. 147.

51. D. J. Wiseman, "The Assyrians," in Hackett, *Warfare in the Ancient World*, p. 48. These techniques were later inherited by the Persians

and later still used by other ancient peoples, including the Greeks and Romans, whose own siegecraft inspired that of medieval European warlords and military engineers.

52. Quoted in Luckenbill, *Ancient Records of Assyria and Babylonia,* vol. 1, p. 223.

53. Roux, *Ancient Iraq,* p. 283.

Chapter 4: Sargon and His Heirs: The Assyrian Empire at Its Height

54. Wolfram von Soden, *The Ancient Orient: An Introduction to the Study of the Ancient Near East.* Translated by Donald G. Schley. Grand Rapids, MI: William B. Eerdmans, 1994, pp. 57–58.

55. Quoted in Luckenbill, *Ancient Records of Assyria and Babylonia,* vol. 2, pp. 74–75.

56. Quoted in Luckenbill, *Ancient Records of Assyria and Babylonia,* vol. 2, p. 82.

57. Years later, after having managed finally to conquer Babylonia, Sargon removed from the city of Uruk the Babylonian chronicle describing his earlier defeat, replacing it with his own, fabricated version of the event. He proceeded to hide the Babylonian account in Nimrud, an act that, ironically, ensured that the truth would one day come out; for modern excavators found it there among the masses of Assyrian records.

58. A. T. Olmstead, *History of Assyria.* Chicago: University of Chicago Press, 1968, pp. 271, 274–75.

59. Quoted in Luckenbill, *Ancient Records of Assyria and Babylonia,* vol. 2, p. 45.

60. By this time, Israel, Judah's Jewish sister-state (originally situated directly north of Judah), had fallen (to Shalamaneser V or perhaps to his successor, Sargon). Thousands of Israelis had been deported and resettled in Assyria, and their homeland had been transformed into a new Assyrian province with Samaria (north of Jerusalem) as its capital.

61. *Annals of Sennacherib,* quoted in Luckenbill, *Ancient Records of Assyria and Babylonia,* vol. 2, p. 152.

62. 2nd Chronicles, in Bible, 32:10–13.

63. Roberta L. Harris, *The World of the Bible.* London: Thames and Hudson, 1995, p. 93.

64. He increased the city's circumference from two to eight miles, widened the town squares, and paved the streets.

65. Quoted in Luckenbill, *Ancient Records of Assyria and Babylonia,* vol. 2, p. 183. Sennacherib's annals go into considerable and often fascinating detail about the rebuilding of both the city and the palace. See Luckenbill, vol. 2, pp. 160–83.

66. *Annals of Esarhaddon,* quoted in Luckenbill, *Ancient Records of Assyria and Babylonia,* vol. 2, pp. 202–203.

67. *Annals of Esarhaddon,* quoted in Luckenbill, *Ancient Records of Assyria and Babylonia,* vol. 2, p. 244.

68. Quoted in Luckenbill, *Ancient Records of Assyria and Babylonia,* vol. 2, p. 227.

69. Quoted in Luckenbill, *Ancient Records of Assyria and Babylonia,* vol. 2, p. 293.

70. Quoted in Oppenheim, *Letters from Mesopotamia,* p. 169.

71. Quoted in Leroy Waterman, *Royal Correspondence of the Assyrian Empire.* 4 vols. Ann Arbor: University of Michigan Press, 1930–1936, vol. 2, p. 365.

72. Nahum, in Bible, 3:7, 15, 19.

Chapter 5: A Society Subservient to Gods and Kings: Assyrian Life and Culture

73. L. Delaporte, *Mesopotamia: The Babylonian and Assyrian Civilization.* Translated by V. Gordon Childe. New York: Barnes and Noble, 1970, pp. 339–40.

74. Roux, *Ancient Iraq,* p. 312.

75. Oppenheim, *Ancient Mesopotamia,* p. 100.

76. Quoted in Luckenbill, *Ancient Records of Assyria and Babylonia,* vol. 2, p. 379.

77. Quoted in Roux, *Ancient Iraq,* p. 315.

78. Quoted in Oppenheim, *Letters from Mesopotamia,* pp. 179–80.

79. Snell, *Life in the Ancient Near East,* p. 122.

80. Snell, *Life in the Ancient Near East,* pp. 122–24.

81. For an excellent, informative, and very readable discussion of building materials, tools, and methods and how they were used in houses, palaces, temples, canals, and more, see L. Sprague de Camp, *The Ancient Engineers.* New York: Ballantine Books, 1963, specifically, "The Mesopotamian Engineers," pp. 46–82.

82. Georges Contenau, *Everyday Life in Babylon and Assyria.* London: Edward Arnold, 1964, pp. 15–17.

83. Chester G. Starr, *A History of the Ancient World.* New York: Oxford University Press, 1991, p. 135.

84. Roux, *Ancient Iraq,* pp. 336–37.

85. Because their goal was to foretell the future, rather than to learn about the true natures of the heavenly bodies, these early observers are perhaps more accurately termed astrologers than astronomers; the first true astronomers were the Greek thinkers of the sixth and fifth centuries B.C.

Chapter 6: A Colossus with Feet of Clay: Assyria's Sudden Collapse

86. Roux, *Ancient Iraq,* p. 294.

87. Quoted in Luckenbill, *Ancient Records of Assyria and Babylonia,* vol. 2, p. 412.

88. Quoted in Luckenbill, *Ancient Records of Assyria and Babylonia,* vol. 2, p. 417.

89. Quoted in Laessoe, *People of Ancient Assyria,* pp. 117–18.

90. Herodotus, 1.99–100, in *Histories,* pp. 82–83.

91. Quoted in Luckenbill, *Ancient Records of Assyria and Babylonia,* vol. 2, pp. 418–19.

92. Quoted in Luckenbill, *Ancient Records of Assyria and Babylonia,* vol. 2, pp. 419–20.

93. Nahum, in Bible, 2:1–10.

94. Quoted in Luckenbill, *Ancient Records of Assyria and Babylonia,* vol. 2, pp. 420–21.

95. Quoted in Olmstead, *History of Assyria,* p. 640.

96. Zephaniah, in Bible, 2:13–15.

Epilogue: A Past That Did Not Die

97. Harris, *World of the Bible,* p. 97.

98. Herodotus, 1.74, in *Histories,* p. 70.

99. Herodotus, 1.74–75, in *Histories,* p. 70.

100. Snell, *Life in the Ancient Near East,* p. 143.

For Further Reading

Michael W. Davison, ed., *Everyday Life Through the Ages*. London: Reader's Digest Association, 1992. This large, beautifully illustrated volume, which examines the way people lived in various cultures throughout history, has a section on ancient Assyria, as well as sections on ancient Babylonia, Persia, and Greece.

Samuel N. Kramer, *Cradle of Civilization*. New York: Time Incorporated, 1967. Written by one of the world's foremost scholars of Mesopotamian culture and lavishly illustrated with stunning photos and drawings, this remains one of the very best basic presentations of Mesopotamian civilization for general readers.

Hazel M. Martell, *The Ancient World: From the Ice Age to the Fall of Rome*. New York: Kingfisher, 1995. A very handsomely mounted book that briefly examines the various important ancient civilizations, including many of those mentioned in this volume about ancient Assyria.

Don Nardo, *The Persian Empire*. San Diego: Lucent Books, 1997. This is in a sense the sequel to the present volume on Assyria; it begins with the destruction of Nineveh and other important Assyrian cities by the Babylonians and Medes and then chronicles the rise and two-century-long reign of the Persians, who based many of their military and administrative customs on those of Assyria.

Chester G. Starr, *Early Man: Prehistory and the Civilizations of the Ancient Near East*. New York: Oxford University Press, 1973. A very well organized and useful general overview of the pageant of Near Eastern peoples, from the first hunter-gatherers, through the Sumerians, Babylonians, Egyptians, Assyrians, and Persians, told by a world-class historian.

Tim Wood, *Ancient Wonders*. New York: Penguin Books, 1991. This beautifully illustrated and informative volume examines the most famous buildings and monuments of ancient times, including the Hanging Gardens of Babylon, built by the son of the Babylonian ruler who destroyed the Assyrian Empire once and for all.

Major Works Consulted

Georges Contenau, *Everyday Life in Babylon and Assyria*. London: Edward Arnold, 1964. Contenau, distinguished Assyriologist, concentrates on the period of circa 700 to 530 B.C., encompassing Assyria and Babylonia at their heights, partly because it is representative of these cultures and also because it is their most documented period. He covers diverse aspects of society, including home life, marriage, farming, trade, religion, literature, entertainment, and much more.

Sir John Hackett, ed., *Warfare in the Ancient World*. New York: Facts On File, 1989. This extremely informative and handsome volume is a collection of long, detailed essays by world-class historians, each of whom tackles the military development and methods of a single ancient people or empire. The beautiful and accurate illustrations are by the famous scholar-artist Peter Connolly. Of main interest for the purposes of this volume on the Assyrian Empire are "The Beginnings of Warfare" (pp. 15–35), by Dr. Trevor Watkins, of the Archaeology Department at Edinburgh University, who summarizes the weapons and tactics of the Sumerians and other early Near Eastern peoples; and "The Assyrians" (pp. 36–53), by D. J. Wiseman, the distinguished Assyriologist at the University of London, who examines in detail the fearsome military machine that terrorized the Near East and significantly influenced the later Persian military.

Holy Bible. Revised Standard Version. New York: Thomas Nelson and Sons, 1952. The Bible contains numerous references to the Assyrians (especially in the books of Isaiah, Ezekiel, Kings, Chronicles, and Nahum) and other Near Eastern peoples with whom they interacted. Although not straightforward historical chronicles, these tracts preserve valuable information about people, customs, and events of the Near East in the first millennium B.C., data that historians attempt to correlate with Assyrian and Babylonian chronicles and archaeological finds.

Jorgen Laessoe, *People of Ancient Assyria: Their Inscriptions and Correspondence*. Translated by F. S. Leigh-Browne. London: Routledge and Kegan Paul, 1963. A worthwhile overview of Assyrian history, concentrating a great deal more space to and analysis of the eighteenth-century B.C. dynasty of King Shamshi-Adad than most other similar studies; supported by numerous long primary source quotes.

Daniel D. Luckenbill, ed., *Ancient Records of Assyria and Babylonia*. 2 vols. Chicago: University of Chicago Press, 1926. Reprint: New York: Greenwood Press, 1968. This set is among a handful of major compilations of English translations of ancient Assyrian and Babylonian annals, letters, inscriptions, and other documents routinely consulted and quoted by scholars and serious students of Mesopotamian civilization. Among the others I have used in writing this book are A. Leo Oppenheim's *Letters from Mesopotamia: Official, Business, and Private Letters on Clay Tablets from Two Millennia*. Chicago: University of Chicago Press, 1967; and Leroy Waterman's *Royal Correspondence of the Assyrian Empire*. 4 vols. Ann Arbor: University of Michigan Press, 1930–1936.

A. T. Olmstead, *History of Assyria*. Chicago: University of Chicago Press, 1923. Reprints: 1960, 1968. This massive (655 pages) and authoritative volume by the late Professor Olmstead, one of the preeminent Near Eastern scholars of the first half of the twentieth century, is now somewhat dated; however, it remains an important and useful reference guide for scholars, despite its dry and ponderous writing style. His *History of the Persian Empire* (Chicago: University of Chicago Press, 1948. Reprints: 1959, 1984) is equally authoritative, less dated, but unfortunately no less ponderous.

A. Leo Oppenheim, *Ancient Mesopotamia: Portrait of a Dead Civilization*. Chicago: University of Chicago Press, 1977. A highly detailed, well-written, and informative discussion of Mesopotamian culture by one of the recognized masters in the field.

Andre Parrot, *Arts of Assyria*. New York: Golden Press, 1961. A lavishly illustrated presentation of the works of Assyrian artists. One of the best of its kind.

Georges Roux, *Ancient Iraq*. New York: Penguin, 1980. An extremely comprehensive and well-written overview of Mesopotamian history and culture, from the prehistoric period, through the rise and fall of the major peoples who dominated the region—the Sumerians, Babylonians, Assyrians, Persians, Hellenistic Greeks, and Parthians. Highly recommended for serious students of the subject.

Daniel C. Snell, *Life in the Ancient Near East, 3100–332 B.C.* New Haven, CT: Yale University Press, 1997. This sweeping overview of Near Eastern culture, customs, and ideas by Professor Snell, of the University of Oklahoma, is up-to-date, briskly written, informative, and copiously documented. Highly recommended.

Additional Works Consulted

Maria E. Aubert, *The Phoenicians and the West*. Translated by Mary Turton. New York: Columbia University Press, 1993.

Paul G. Bahn, ed., *The Cambridge Illustrated History of Archaeology*. New York: Cambridge University Press, 1996.

Nels M. Bailkey, ed., *Readings in Ancient History: From Gilgamesh to Diocletian*. Lexington, MA: D. C. Heath, 1976.

James Henry Breasted, *Ancient Times: A History of the Early World*. Boston: Ginn and Company, 1944.

C. W. Ceram, *Gods, Graves, and Scholars: The Story of Archaeology*. Translated by E. B. Garside and Sophie Wilkins. New York: Random House, 1986.

L. Delaporte, *Mesopotamia: The Babylonian and Assyrian Civilization*. Translated by V. Gordon Childe. New York: Barnes and Noble, 1970.

Robert Drews, *The Coming of the Greeks: Indo-European Conquests in the Aegean and the Near East*. Princeton, NJ: Princeton University Press, 1988.

———, *The End of the Bronze Age: Changes in Warfare and the Catastrophe ca. 1200 B.C.* Princeton, NJ: Princeton University Press, 1993.

Henri Frankfort, *Art and Architecture of the Ancient Orient*. New York: Penguin, 1971.

A. Kirk Grayson, *Assyrian Rulers of the Third and Second Millennia B.C.* Toronto: University of Toronto Press, 1987.

Roberta L. Harris, *The World of the Bible*. London: Thames and Hudson, 1995.

Herodotus, *The Histories*. Translated by Aubrey de Selincourt. New York: Penguin, 1972.

Tom B. Jones, ed., *The Sumerian Problem*. New York: John Wiley, 1969.

John Keegan, *A History of Warfare*. New York: Random House, 1993.

Samuel N. Kramer, *The Sumerians: Their History, Culture and Character*. Chicago: University of Chicago Press, 1971.

Seton Lloyd, *Foundations in the Dust*. New York: Thames and Hudson, 1981.

James B. Pritchard, ed., *Ancient Near Eastern Texts Relating to the Old Testament*. Princeton, NJ: Princeton University Press, 1969.

John M. Russell, *Sennacherib's Palace Without Rival at Nineveh*. Chicago: University of Chicago Press, 1991.

H. W. F. Saggs, *Civilization Before Greece and Rome*. New Haven, CT: Yale University Press, 1989.

Chester G. Starr, *A History of the Ancient World*. New York: Oxford University Press, 1991.

Wolfram von Soden, *The Ancient Orient: An Introduction to the Study of the Ancient Near East*. Translated by Donald G. Schley. Grand Rapids, MI: William B. Eerdmans, 1994.

Michael Wood, *Legacy: The Search for Ancient Cultures*. New York: Sterling Publishing, 1992.

C. Leonard Woolley, *The Sumerians*. New York: W. W. Norton, 1965.

Index

Picture Credits

About the Author

Classical historian and award-winning writer Don Nardo has published more than twenty books about the ancient world. These include general histories, such as *The Persian Empire, Philip and Alexander: The Unification of Greece,* and *The Decline and Fall of Rome;* war chronicles, such as *The Punic Wars* and *The Battle of Marathon;* cultural studies, such as *Life in Ancient Greece, Greek and Roman Theater, Life as a Roman Slave,* and *The Trial of Socrates;* and literary companions to the works of Homer and Sophocles. Mr. Nardo also writes screenplays and teleplays and composes music. He lives with his lovely wife, Christine, and dog Bud on Cape Cod, Massachusetts.